# Fundamentals of Compliance

**By James R Downing**

# Acknowledgements

First and foremost, I want to thank all of the wonderful people and organizations I have worked with as a regulator and Compliance professional over the past 20+ years. Without your insight, assistance and guidance, I would not have been able to formulate the Fundamentals of Compliance. A special thank you to Adam Leber for helping me with the outline of the book before I ever began writing. I would also like to thank my family for putting up with me while writing this. It was a dream of mine to write this book and I would not have been able to do it without my wife, Adria, and my kids, Sophie and Paul.

# Forward:

James Downing has written an excellent book on the Fundamentals of Compliance. I would encourage all compliance professional to read this book. Whether you are new to compliance or a seasoned expert, it provides a comprehensive end to end guidance on practical solutions to implement effective and efficient compliance practices. In that spirit, it would be equally valuable to directors on boards overseeing compliance, teachers and students engaged in the study of compliance, and regulatory professionals looking to better understand industry best practices in complying with the letter and the spirit of laws, regulations and ethical standards. All readers will learn valuable lessons in how to improve the effectiveness and efficiency of their organization's compliance programs.

It doesn't surprise me that James has taken the time and effort to document such thoughtful guidance. I had the pleasure of meeting James when he was Chairman of the Board of the National Society of Compliance Professionals (NSCP) and I was serving on the NSCP's Regulatory Advisory Committee, after serving a decade in senior regulatory roles at the SEC and FINRA. His commitment to the compliance mission, compliance profession, and compliance education was clear to me then. It is even more clear and compelling now, as I appreciate the care and thought that James has poured into this book to create a valuable resource for the compliance profession.

In this book, James guides the reader in a clear conversational manner through the fundamentals of risk assessment, policies and training, monitoring and testing, issues and exams, governance and reporting, and the importance of practical advice. In each chapter, he clearly explains the fundamental principles and sets forth helpful examples so the practitioner can both understand and apply effective practices. He also clarifies roles and responsibilities and provides guidance on effective teamwork and collaboration across different roles in the organization, so that stakeholders can drive better compliance outcomes across their organization.

Finally, as a former senior executive at both the SEC and FINRA, and as the Global Advisory Leader at ACA, I care deeply about investor protection, market integrity and capital formation. Helping firms implement effective and efficient compliance programs is not only critical to helping firms launch, grow and protect their businesses, but it is also critical to supporting investor protection, market integrity and capital formation in our economy and markets more broadly. As compliance professionals read and apply the fundamental principles and guidance in this book they are not only strengthening compliance, but they are also doing their part to strengthen investor protection, market integrity and capital formation.

Carlo di Florio, Global Advisory Leader, ACA Group

<u>Carlo di Florio Bio</u>

Carlo di Florio is the Global Advisory Leader at ACA Group. ACA supports over 6,500 clients with Governance, Risk and Compliance (GRC) advisory, technology, outsourcing and data analytics solutions. Prior to joining ACA in 2019, Carlo served for a decade as a senior regulator, first as the Director of the SEC's Division of Compliance Inspections and Examinations (OCIE, now the Division of Examinations) and then as the Chief Risk and Strategy Officer at the Financial Industry Regulatory Authority (FINRA). Prior to joining the SEC in 2010, in the wake of the Financial Crisis, Carlo was a Partner at PricewaterhouseCoopers (PwC) in the Financial Services Risk and Regulatory Practice. Carlo served as co-President and currently serves as Governor of the Risk Management Association (RMA) NY Chapter. He also serves on the Regulatory Advisory Committee of the National Association of Compliance Professionals (NSCP) and on the Board of Advisors of the Private Equity CFO Association NY Chapter (PECFOA). In addition, Carlo serves as a Lecturer at Columbia University, where he teaches

Strategic Risk Management in the Masters of Science program in Enterprise Risk Management.

# Table of Contents

# Introduction to "The Fundamentals of Compliance"

## Why Compliance?

In almost every organization across the globe, regardless of the industry, compliance plays a critical role. Compliance stands as a universal pillar in every organization worldwide, transcending industry boundaries. Whether in finance, healthcare, technology, or manufacturing, adherence to laws, regulations, and ethical standards is not merely a legal formality but a fundamental aspect of operational integrity and reputation. As businesses operate in increasingly complex environments with stringent regulatory demands, the role of compliance has never been more crucial. It ensures that organizations not only prevent costly legal violations but also foster a culture of transparency and accountability. This sets the stage for a discussion on the pivotal role of compliance in sustaining business operations and driving long-term success while implementing the Fundamentals of Compliance.

Reflecting on the past quarter-century, the ascension of the compliance profession underscores a shift in corporate culture—from a peripheral consideration to a central, strategic function. Decades ago, as a college student, the realm of compliance was not just unfamiliar to me—it was virtually non-existent in the formal job market. Compliance duties were often relegated to the margins of roles in legal, accounting, operations, or other departments, handled almost as an afterthought. Today, however, the landscape is vastly different. Compliance professionals have emerged as pivotal figures in ensuring that organizations not only adhere to legal and ethical standards but thrive because of them.

Throughout my career in financial services, I have cultivated a deep understanding of compliance, though the principles I've come to know are not confined to any single sector. Whether in financial services, healthcare, education, technology, or beyond, the Fundamentals of Compliance form the backbone of an effective compliance program. This book distills these insights into five fundamental aspects: risk assessments, policies, procedures and training, monitoring and testing, issues and exams, and reporting. All centered around advice. Below is an illustration:

Designed to offer a comprehensive overview, this book aims to outline what a robust compliance program looks like in practice.

## Why Write This Book?

After more than two decades in financial services, and witnessing firsthand the transformative impact of well-implemented compliance frameworks, I felt compelled to share my knowledge. "The Fundamentals of Compliance" is crafted to demystify the core practices that underpin an effective compliance department. My intention is to transcend industry boundaries, offering a primer that is universally applicable, easy to understand, and foundational. This book is not an exhaustive manual but rather an accessible guide meant for every compliance professional —from seasoned compliance officers to those new to the field.

Amidst the constantly evolving regulatory environment marked by rapid changes in technology and market dynamics, a static approach to compliance is insufficient. This book aims to establish a dynamic framework that is adaptable across different industries and responsive to the inevitable shifts in regulatory landscapes. By doing so, it seeks to support aspiring compliance officers and industry professionals in designing and sustaining effective compliance programs.

## Who is This Book For?

"Fundamentals of Compliance" is designed for anyone operating within a regulated environment. You might wonder, "Is my industry regulated?" Consider this: if there are state, local or federal regulations that impact how your organization operates, then you are part of a regulated industry. In truth, very few sectors escape regulation at some level—be it local, state, or federal.

This book serves as a straightforward, practical guide to understanding the fundamentals of a compliance program. Written in plain English and crafted for ease of understanding, it addresses the needs of a diverse audience. Whether you are a seasoned professional seeking to refine your understanding or a newcomer aiming to grasp the basics, this book aims to equip you with the foundational knowledge necessary to navigate the complexities of compliance.

As you embark on this journey through "The Fundamentals of Compliance," I invite you to engage with this material not just as educational but as a roadmap to excellence in compliance practices. The fundamentals outlined here are intended to be foundational yet adaptable, providing a baseline from which your understanding and practices can evolve as the profession and industry landscapes shift.

# Risk Assessment

## What is a Risk Assessment?

A risk assessment is a critical element of an effective compliance program. There is a reason the fundamentals start with risk assessments as its the core on which all compliance programs are built. It provides a structured approach to identifying, evaluating, and mitigating risks associated with non-compliance to regulatory and legal obligations. The evolving landscape of regulations across various industries underscores the increasing importance of a systematic and proactive approach to compliance. This introductory section will explore the significance of risk assessments, discuss the evolution of risk management in the context of compliance, and provide basic guidance on how a risk assessment can be designed and executed.

Foundational to any compliance program is the method by which a risk assessment is conducted. The ability of a compliance professional to objectively analyze rules, regulations, and policy against the subsequent controls allows an organization to determine where compliance risk lives within an organization. What this isn't is a comprehensive risk assessment across a firm. A good compliance program is responsible for conducting a regulatory risk assessment. This means that certain areas, operation risk, market risk, liquidity risk, etc., should not be included unless covered by a specific rule or regulation. Compliance is responsible for tracking regulatory risk. While it can be combined with other risk assessments, and often is, it should not be the burden of compliance to conduct a risk assessment outside of these areas. This chapter will focus on many different areas of risk assessment, methodology, identifying risk, measuring risk, collaboration, reporting, and regulatory change management.

A comprehensive risk assessment process enables organizations to not only detect and mitigate existing risks but also to anticipate emerging ones. By understanding the full spectrum of their regulatory obligations, organizations can allocate resources more effectively, implement appropriate controls, and reduce the likelihood of non-compliance.

This process in a compliance program is truly foundational and should not be taken lightly. A lot of thought should go into the design and implementation of a risk assessment as it has broad implications across an organization. Every compliance program should start with a risk assessment. It is the practice that ties all of the other fundamentals together. Without this step, a compliance program would be considered ineffective at best. This chapter is the key to this program. Without it, the rest of the Fundamentals of Compliance do not work. For example, a compliance risk assessment should be used to design and write policies across the organization. Without the risk assessment, an organization may not have policies for a specific regulatory risk, for example sanctions compliance, and be exposing themselves to potential fines, censures and negative press.

## Methodology

Determining the methodology for the design and implementation of a risk assessment is one of the most important aspects of a compliance program and should not be done with haste. Careful thought should be made into how the risk assessment will be conducted, who will be completing it, in which format, and ultimately, how it will be reported. All of these will be covered below and will depend on the type of organization and the industry in which it operates. Whatever methodology you determine is right for your compliance program risk assessment, it is important that it be documented. This can usually be done by writing out the rationale behind why you chose to conduct your risk assessment in a certain manner. Getting buy-in on the methodology before it's adopted is also important. Make sure senior leaders within the organization approve of the method you are using.

A risk assessment breaks analysis into two key components: inherent risk and control effectiveness. This gives you the residual risk (discussed in more detail later). When designing a risk assessment methodology, you should also be aware that the execution will result in a considerable expense of time. This is key in the design process, as launching a risk assessment that which the organization does not have the capacity to complete will result in frustration and distrust.

## Key Theories and Models in Risk Assessment

Risk assessment in compliance relies on several theoretical models that provide a framework for understanding and managing risks. Notable among these are:

1. **The Risk Management Standard (ISO 31000)** - This international standard provides guidelines on risk management principles and implementation, emphasizing a structured approach to compliance.

2. **COSO Framework for Enterprise Risk Management** - Widely accepted in the United States, the COSO framework integrates risk management into the broader strategy and operations, focusing on performance, reporting, and compliance.

3. **The Basel Accords** - Specifically influential in the banking sector, these accords provide a set of international banking regulations on bank capital risk, market risk, and operational risk.

Each model offers different perspectives and tools for assessing and managing risk, and their application can vary depending on the regulatory environment and industry specifics.

The application of these theories in compliance programs involves adapting their general principles to the specific needs and challenges of regulatory compliance. For instance:

- **ISO 31000** helps organizations develop a risk management strategy that aligns with overall corporate objectives and compliance requirements.

- **COSO's ERM Framework** is particularly useful in integrating risk management with compliance by ensuring that organizational governance is robust enough to anticipate and mitigate compliance risks.

- **The Basel Accords** require banks to maintain sufficient capital and implement rigorous risk assessment procedures to manage and minimize risk exposure effectively.

Work to become familiar with each of these standards as they are well-accepted practices across the globe. In some jurisdictions, other risk assessment frameworks exist. Even if outside of your industry, becoming familiar with regulatory expectations outside of your industry can assist you in building the right methodology. This section will delve into the practical implications of deploying these models within an organization's compliance framework, including how they can be tailored to enhance compliance programs and what benefits they offer in terms of improved risk visibility and management.

## Rules Based vs. Thematic

First, lets talk about creating a risk assessment that is rules based. As with anything, there are pros and cons to doing it this way. A rules-based risk assessment breaks down every regulatory and/or policy requirement and assesses it based on inherent risk and control effectiveness. While this process is the most thorough, it may not be the most efficient use of time in the organization. Thus, you should consider whether a rules-based approach is appropriate for your organization. Some things to consider should be:

- The size of your organization

- Compliance department capacity

- The level at which your organization is regulated (e.g. one regulator or multiple)

- The number of jurisdictions in which you operate

- The organizations customer base (B2C vs. B2B)

Rules-based risk assessments are very detailed and usually meet all regulatory requirements. They can have detailed descriptions of controls, policies, risk owners, and more. However, some of the drawbacks are that they are incredibly difficult to execute on, given they are more lengthy and detailed. Additionally, summarizing results for senior management or other leaders, including potential regulators, can sometimes be difficult. If you are subject to over 100 rules or regulations, you may want to consider another method, thematic.

Thematic based risk assessments bunch together various risks into themes that apply across an organization. This is extremely helpful if your organization is highly complex, has multiple regulated entities, or spans several jurisdictions. Examples of common themes include:

- Privacy

- Anti-Money Laundering

- Bribery, corruption and sanctions

- Marketing

- Anti-fraud and sales practices

- Customer disclosure

- Regulatory reporting

- Cyber security

- Third party risk management

Of course this list is not exhaustive. It will depend on your organization, the type of business it conducts and the jurisdictions in which it operates. Thematic risk assessments allow for collaboration across multiple jurisdictions in several different business units. Another advantage is that they are generally easy to repurpose for reporting to senior management and regulators.

Disadvantages of using a thematic approach is it may be too general or vague. Also thematic risk assessment which encompass multiple entities need to be weighted appropriately so that a small aspect of the business would not unfairly throw off the overall residual risk rating.

Overall, the approach needs to be tailored to your organizational needs and requirements. From experience working at large organizations, thematic risk assessments were effective, but specific business units still prepared rules-based risk assessments for their own needs. This is entirely up to the people designing the methodology and how comprehensive they want to make it. There is no one right way to conduct a compliance risk assessment. Be mindful not to over-engineer the methodology. This will create complexity where it is not needed and make it difficult to execute.

# Format

The format of the risk assessment is entirely up to the team designing it. Automation and the use of equations to calculate residual risk are preferred, but it can also be done manually. There are many software providers in the market who also provide this service. These vendors have generally improved in the 20+ years I have been in the market. I am not going to recommend one or talk about any one provider.

Modern compliance programs often employ various tools and technologies to assist in risk assessments, such as:

- **Compliance Management Software**: These platforms can track changes in regulations and alert compliance officers to potential new risks.

- **Data Analytics**: Advanced analytics can help identify patterns that might indicate areas of potential non-compliance.

- **Artificial Intelligence (AI)**: AI can be used to predict and identify risks by analyzing large volumes of data more efficiently than traditional methods.

If you have the budget to use compliance management software, I would suggest making sure any vendor can accommodate your organizations particular needs. Off-the-shelf systems can look great but, in practice can be rigid in focus and create inefficiency.

It is also possible to do this in a tool like Microsoft Excel or Word. Again it's going to be entirely up to you. Remember that whatever is created should be somewhat flexible for future changes. As new regulations emerge or the organization enters new markets, it is important for all of this to be reflected in the risk assessment. Risk assessments are not static documents but also must be stored once finalized. Risk assessments should at least be revised annually, so the format should be considered when taking this into consideration. Below is an example of using excel:

| Risk | Inherent Risk | Control Effectiveness | Residual Risk |
| --- | --- | --- | --- |
| Data Breach (Privacy) | High | Medium | High |
| Regulatory Non-compliance (AML) | Medium | High | Low |
| Reputational Risk (Marketing/Sales) | High | Low | High |

You may also want to add columns for notes, description of control, risk owner, etc. This illustration is for example purposes only.

## Identifying Risk

Whether you take a rules-based or thematic approach, identifying the regulatory risks associated with your firm should be a thought-driven process. Regulations exist for many organizations at a local or government level. Identify who your regulators are and what rules apply. This can sometimes mean reaching out to resources outside of your organization, such as legal counsel or consultants. Identifying which risks apply is a key responsibility for compliance. Missing something could make your organization subject to regulatory scrutiny or fines.

Take into consideration which products you offer, the organization's client base (e.g. B2C or B2B) and where they are located, the footprint of offices and employees, the location of affiliates, suppliers and vendors, and where the entity may be registered with a regulatory body or subject to its jurisdiction.

Once a list has been compiled it should also be socialized with other leaders within the company. Check to make sure you are not missing something but also listen as they may have insight on products or jurisdictions to which you were unaware. Use the effort of socialization to get buy-in from key counterparties within the organization as to which rules and regulations apply. This will help you build trust in the latter part of execution when sharing results.

## Measuring Risk

The process of measuring inherent risk and control effectiveness is important in the execution phase of completing a risk assessment. Below, I will briefly discuss how to make these determinations without getting too technical. To some, this is a devoted science. To others, it may be an art form. My advice is to take into consideration both qualitative and quantitative data and information when making this assessment. These determinations will have an impact on how your residual risk is calculated. The residual risk is generally what determines other aspects of your overall compliance program, such as monitoring and testing.

## Inherent Risk

In its most basic form the inherent risk is the liability to an organization for non-compliance with a rule or regulation if there were *no controls in place*. This can sometimes be a difficult ideal to consider. As an example, if your organization was processing or collecting personal information from individuals and had no controls around Privacy it could be subject to huge fines, negative press, and potentially lawsuits. When determining inherent risk take into consideration the following factors:

- The level/volume at which your organization engages in this activity

- The potential penalties and fines for non-compliance

- Whether the regulation is complex in nature

- Whether there have been other companies subject to enforcement actions or penalties

- Whether the Regulator considers compliance with this rule to be a priority

There may be other factors to consider, but these will get you thinking about the inherent risk. Inherent risk should be rated on a scale. A basic rating consists of high, medium or low. Of course, you could use a 5 or 10-point scale but given the size and complexity of your organization, I would also caution about over-engineering this rating scale. Making it too complex could create problems. Make sure you have buy-in from senior management on how risks will be rated. All ratings should be well defined in a methodology and those definitions should be documented and shared.

## Control Effectiveness

Determining the control effectiveness takes into consideration different factors, the presence of a control to prevent non-compliance, and known issues or breaches with compliance. First it is important to document what controls exist. Examples of controls may be:

- Training on a policy

- A formal quality assurance review process

- Compliance monitoring or testing

- Internal or external audit testing

- Access controls to data or information

- Audit trails

- Vendor due diligence processes

- Reporting - internally or to regulators

These are only some examples. You will notice that compliance policies are not listed. A policy is generally not a control unless employees have been adequately trained on its requirements. Identifying the specific control, or controls (there could be multiple), is important because it will impact the control effectiveness rating assigned. As important is identifying known issues or breaches. This is more quantifiable in nature and less qualitative. Having good data around known issues and or breaches will assist you in making a determination if the control is effective. If a system or process is known to break down frequently, then the control cannot be deemed effective.

Having a rating scale here is generally simpler than inherent risk. I would suggest the following:

- Effective: the control has no breakdowns and no known issues or breaches

- Partially effective: the controls are known to have some breakdowns but not more than 20%

- Not effective: the control has frequent breakdowns (more than 20%) and is not reliable

- No Control in place: there are no known controls in place

These ratings are subject to interpretation and the compliance team must define what parameters they wish to use when calculating residual risk. Avoid the urge to overcomplicate this, keeping it simple will mean its easier to communicate the methodology.

## Residual Risk

Residual risk is calculated by taking the inherent risk and incorporating the effectiveness of controls. For example, in the instance of Privacy regulations you might determine the inherent risk is high. However the controls identified are numerous and are known to be effective. Thus, the residual risk might be moderate or medium (using a 5-point scale).

Here is a proposed table to illustrate how these interactions might work:

| Inherent Risk | Control Effectiveness | Residual Risk |
| --- | --- | --- |
| Low | Effective | Very Low |
| Low | Partially Effective | Low |
| Low | Not Effective | Medium |

| Medium | Effective | Low |
| --- | --- | --- |
| Medium | Partially Effective | Medium |
| Medium | Not Effective | High |
| High | Effective | Medium |
| High | Partially Effective | High |
| High | Not Effective | Very High |

Description:

1. **Very Low**: The risk is almost negligible, and controls are very effective.

2. **Low**: Risk is minor and generally manageable.

3. **Medium**: Risk is moderate needs regular review and management.

4. **High**: Risk is considerable, may require additional controls or mitigation strategies.

5. **Very High**: Risk is severe and immediate action is required.

This table is a basic framework. Depending on specific circumstances, organizational risk tolerance, and the environment, the actual calculation and categorization of risk may require more detailed analysis and could involve more sophisticated risk assessment models.

# Collaboration

Collaboration is key in conducting an effective compliance risk assessment. Involving various departments ensures that all potential risks are identified and accurately evaluated. Different teams within an organization often have unique insights into specific challenges and regulatory requirements that affect their operations. For example, the IT department may highlight cybersecurity risks, while the finance team might pinpoint compliance issues related to fiscal reporting. By fostering a collaborative environment, organizations can create a comprehensive risk assessment that encompasses diverse perspectives, enhancing the overall accuracy and reliability of the findings. This approach not only broadens the understanding of potential risks but also aids in developing more robust strategies for managing these risks. This process cannot take place in a vacuum. Compliance needs to ensure collaboration when identifying controls and assessing their effectiveness.

Gaining buy-in from senior management is crucial for the successful implementation of compliance measures identified through the risk assessment process. When senior leaders endorse the compliance program, it sends a strong message across the organization about the importance of adhering to legal and regulatory standards. Their support not only allocates the necessary resources, such as funding and manpower but also significantly influences the organizational culture, encouraging employees at all levels to take compliance seriously. Senior management's active involvement in the compliance process helps to align the strategic objectives of the compliance program with the broader goals of the organization, ensuring a unified approach to managing risk.

Moreover, when senior management is involved from the onset of the compliance risk assessment, it facilitates a smoother implementation of necessary changes and compliance strategies. Their understanding of the strategic implications of compliance risks enables them to make informed decisions that can preemptively mitigate potential legal or financial penalties. Additionally, their visible commitment to compliance strengthens the organization's reputation both internally and externally, enhancing stakeholder trust and confidence. Hence, their early and ongoing engagement is indispensable not only for the alignment of compliance with business strategies but also for reinforcing a culture of compliance throughout the organization.

## Reporting

Reporting the results of compliance risk assessments is a crucial step in ensuring that an organization remains in alignment with both internal standards and external regulatory requirements. Effective reporting acts as a bridge between the identification of potential risks and the implementation of strategies to manage them. By transparently presenting the findings, stakeholders are kept informed about the current compliance landscape, which supports strategic decision-making. This process not only highlights areas of concern but also showcases areas where the organization performs strongly, providing a balanced view that can guide future investments and policy development.

The concept of "effective challenge" is integral to the reporting process. This involves a critical evaluation of the risk assessment results by individuals who were not directly involved in the initial analysis. The purpose of this challenge is to ensure that the conclusions drawn are robust, justifiable, and free from biases that may have influenced the original assessors. This scrutiny helps in identifying any oversights and confirms the reliability of the findings before they are used to make significant decisions. Effective challenge thus acts as a safeguard against potential errors and ensures that the organization's response to compliance risks is both appropriate and proportionate. Compliance will put in a lot of work to create and report on a risk assessment it is important that you see the effective challenge as a growth opportunity and not become defensive. Be prepared for it and embrace it as a method of strengthening your program.

Documenting the results of a compliance risk assessment thoroughly is another vital aspect of the reporting process. Detailed documentation not only supports transparency and accountability but also provides a legal safeguard for the organization. It serves as a record that the organization is actively managing its compliance responsibilities, which can be crucial during regulatory reviews or audits. Furthermore, comprehensive documentation allows for a historical perspective, enabling the organization to track its progress over time and make adjustments based on past experiences and the ever-evolving regulatory landscapes.

Summarizing the findings of a compliance risk assessment effectively is equally important. A well-crafted summary provides a clear and concise overview of the key risks, their potential impacts, and recommended actions. It allows senior management and relevant stakeholders to quickly grasp critical issues without delving into the more technical details contained in the full report. This summary should be actionable, highlighting priority areas that need immediate attention and suggesting realistic steps for mitigation. Such summaries facilitate quicker decision-making processes and help maintain the momentum of compliance efforts.

Heat maps can often be used to show a graphic representation of a risk assessment. Showing the results of a risk assessment graphically can allow the audience to see information outside of the data. Be prepared with any backup if using graphics, e.g. the actual risk assessment. Graphic examples can also raise questions such as, why is that risk so high? or why is that control ineffective? Be prepared where outliers exist on charts or graphs to explain. Senior management is generally used to seeing information in this format, and it will be much appreciated as opposed to providing them with rows of data or written summaries.

Overall, the importance of reporting the results of compliance risk assessments cannot be understated. Effective reporting, coupled with a robust challenge process, thorough documentation, and clear summarization, ensures that compliance risks are managed proactively and efficiently. These practices not only help safeguard the organization against possible compliance breaches and the resulting penalties but also enhance the organization's reputation by demonstrating a commitment to ethical operations and compliance. Through diligent reporting, organizations can maintain a strong compliance posture that supports sustainable growth and success in a competitive business environment.

## Regulatory Change Management

Compliance tracking of regulatory changes is a critical function for any organization operating in regulated industries. This proactive approach ensures that an organization is always aware of and aligned with current laws and regulations, thereby preventing compliance pitfalls and maintaining its reputation. Regulatory landscapes can shift rapidly due to changes in political climates, advancements in technology, or evolving societal norms, and staying updated with these changes is crucial. An effective tracking process helps organizations anticipate and adapt to these changes efficiently, minimizing the risk of compliance breaches that can lead to hefty fines, compliance challenges, and damaged reputations.

The impact of tracking regulatory changes on compliance risk assessments is profound. As regulations evolve, the parameters of what constitutes a risk also change. Regular updates to compliance programs, informed by the latest regulatory changes, ensure that risk assessments are always relevant and comprehensive. This means not only adapting to new regulations but also re-evaluating existing compliance measures to see if they are still sufficient or if they need enhancement. This dynamic approach to risk assessment helps organizations remain resilient against compliance threats and ensures that they are not caught off-guard by new regulatory requirements.

Moreover, tracking regulatory changes enables organizations to be strategically ahead. By understanding potential regulatory shifts before they are implemented, organizations can prepare and adapt in advance, which provides a competitive advantage. This foresight allows them to allocate resources more effectively, plan strategic responses, and even influence regulatory developments through advocacy and dialogue with regulators. For compliance officers, this proactive approach to managing regulatory changes is a key element of strategic risk management, enabling the organization to navigate through regulatory waters with greater agility and confidence.

In conclusion, the importance of tracking regulatory changes as part of compliance risk management cannot be overemphasized. It ensures that compliance risk assessments are timely, accurate, and effective in identifying and mitigating risks associated with regulatory non-compliance. This proactive tracking not only protects the organization from potential legal and financial penalties but also enhances its ability to operate efficiently and ethically in a complex regulatory environment. For businesses aiming to sustain and grow their operations, investing in robust systems or processes to track and respond to regulatory changes is essential for maintaining a resilient and compliant organizational structure.

## Conclusion

As we conclude this chapter on compliance risk assessments, it is crucial to reflect on the integral role that these assessments play in the strategic management of compliance risks within an organization. The effectiveness of a compliance program hinges significantly on how accurately and thoroughly risks are assessed. This involves selecting the right methodology, identifying applicable risks, measuring these risks, and ensuring efficient reporting and adaptation processes. Each component plays a critical role in fortifying the organization's compliance posture, making compliance risk assessments not just a regulatory necessity but a strategic imperative.

The methodology adopted for risk assessment can significantly influence the effectiveness of a compliance program. A rules-based approach, which is highly structured and specific, focuses on clear, established regulations and the straightforward application of these rules. This method is particularly effective in environments with well-defined regulatory frameworks and where compliance obligations are clear-cut. However, its rigidity can sometimes overlook emerging risks that haven't yet been addressed by existing regulations.

In contrast, a thematic approach offers a more flexible and holistic examination of compliance risks. This method assesses risks across themes or topics, such as cyber security or data protection, which might span multiple regulatory frameworks or operational areas. Thematic assessments are advantageous in dynamic sectors where new risks emerge rapidly and require a proactive approach to identify and mitigate issues before they become entrenched. The choice between these methodologies often depends on the specific industry, the regulatory environment, and the unique operational aspects of the organization.

A critical step in compliance risk assessments is the identification of relevant risks. This process involves understanding the full spectrum of the organization's activities and the external factors affecting it. Compliance officers must have a deep understanding of both the business and the regulatory landscape to pinpoint specific risks that could impact the organization. This phase is pivotal because an oversight here could lead to unaddressed vulnerabilities.

Once risks are identified, measuring them becomes essential. This involves assessing the inherent risk associated with a particular area without considering any controls that may mitigate that risk. Understanding inherent risk provides a baseline level of risk exposure. The next step is to evaluate the effectiveness of existing controls in mitigating those risks. This evaluation helps in determining the residual risk, which is the level of risk remaining after all controls are in place. Regular assessment of both inherent and residual risks is necessary to ensure that controls are both effective and efficient.

Remember that a risk assessment is not a task for the compliance department alone. It requires collaboration across various departments and levels of an organization. Engaging different parts of the organization not only helps in identifying and assessing risks more accurately but also aids in the socialization of the compliance program. This means embedding a culture of compliance throughout the organization, from the boardroom to the frontline employees. Effective socialization ensures that compliance considerations become a part of the decision-making process at all levels.

Effective communication of the outcomes of risk assessments to senior management is crucial. Detailed reports should include both inherent and residual risks, the effectiveness of current controls, and recommendations for mitigation strategies. These reports enable senior management to make informed decisions about where to allocate resources and how to strategically address compliance risks.

In conclusion, compliance risk assessments are a dynamic and complex process integral to the effectiveness of an organization's compliance program. The choice of assessment methodology, the precision in identifying risks, the accuracy in measuring these risks, and the effectiveness of reporting and adapting to changes are all critical to the success of this process. By embedding a culture of regular assessment and adaptation, organizations can not only meet regulatory expectations but also protect themselves from potential compliance failures. This proactive approach to compliance management ensures that the organization not only survives but thrives in the face of regulatory challenges.

# Policies and Training

## Introduction

The field of compliance is crucial for ensuring that organizations adhere to laws, regulations, ethical standards, and internal guidelines. One of the fundamentals of an effective compliance program is the development, communication, and enforcement of clear policies. This chapter will explore the different types of compliance documents that form the backbone of any robust compliance program. Understanding these documents is essential for anyone involved in the creation or management of a compliance program.

Using the risk assessment discussed in the last chapter as a guide to map out regulatory responsibilities and controls, you can begin to develop policies and procedures. There is a difference between a policy and a procedure. A policy generally states a matter of rule. For example do conduct personal stock trades based on inside information. The procedure would outline how the company enforces such a rule, for example monitoring employee personal trading statements to ensure this is not happening. For that reason, you generally want to keep policies and procedures separate. Doing this allows for greater simplicity and lets employees know what is expected of them within company policies.

## Policies

Policies are the foundational documents within an organization that outline the rules, principles, and guidelines employees must follow. They serve as the framework for operational and decision-making processes, ensuring consistency and legality in business operations. This section will discuss how policies are created and the role they play in maintaining organizational integrity and accountability.

## Types of Compliance policies and procedures

i) Code of Conduct

The Code of Conduct is a central guide that communicates the fundamental ethical principles and expectations of an organization. It is designed to provide a comprehensive framework for behavior and decision-making. Every organization should have a code of conduct regardless of size or industry. Expectations for employees should be spelled out clearly and in plain language. Avoid trying to use "big words" and make it so it is easy to understand.

The typical components of a Code of Conduct include ethical standards, conflict of interest policies, and compliance with laws. A general code of conduct will have the following sections:

- Introduction

  - Purpose of the Code of Conduct - this is the "why" it is important to have a code.

  - Importance of ethics and integrity in the organization's operations - all organizations want to conduct business in a lawful and ethical manner. Reinforce this.

  - Scope of the document (to whom it applies to) - This can vary per organization. Some organizations have their code applied to contractors, interns, and even vendors. Of course, you will want to have it be applicable to employees but think of any other individual who may be acting on behalf of the company (e.g. agents or finders) and determine if you want them to abide by the code. Some organizations also create a "Supplier" code of conduct. This should all be considered when drafting.

- Core Values

  - A statement of the organization's core values, such as respect, integrity, responsibility, and excellence - should come from senior leadership at your organization. Values are generally expressed internally and externally, so make sure they are clearly stated and defined.

  - Explanation of how these values guide the organization's policies and practices - this is vital to a code of conduct. The individuals subject to the code will want to know how their role/function aligns with the values of the organization. Many companies like to present values as part of their culture, explaining it in the code helps employees know what is expected of them to align with values.

- Professional Standards

  - Expectations regarding professional behavior - this can include broad-based expectations, for example, honesty and accountability. It can also be very specific, dress code or use of company equipment. While professional behavior is a broad-based term, the code should be direct in this matter.

  - Policies on confidentiality, conflicts of interest, and organizational resources - this is where the "rubber meets the road" in many important aspects, particularly in a regulated industry like financial services where conflicts of interest are harshly scrutinized by regulators. Additionally, the confidentiality of intellectual property and customer data is paramount for any organization to be successful. This section should be very specific in what is allowed and what isn't. It may also contain instructions on reporting things like outside business activities, outside investments, relationships with vendors and other potential conflicts.

- Guidelines on compliance with laws and regulations - while important, many codes point employees to more specific policies in this regard. For example, there may be an insider trading policy that is referenced in the code but not incorporated. This comes down to preference. Some companies may want to include that policy in the code, and others, dependent on complexity, may wish to have it be a stand-alone policy.

- <u>Workplace Environment</u>

  - Policies ensuring a respectful and inclusive workplace - writing these standards should not be done in a bubble. Make sure to reference the employee handbook work with human resources ("HR") and senior management to ensure it aligns with any other company documents. Include broad statements about prohibited behavior but also point to any other document that is more descriptive.

  - Prohibitions against all forms of harassment, discrimination, and violence - make sure to reference the local jurisdiction in this section. Many states, countries, and municipalities have varying laws, and you don't want to be caught off guard by a local requirement. Where you have varying degrees of requirements, a good suggestion is to enforce the most stringent to ensure compliance across all jurisdictions, if applicable. This is also a good section to check with an outside or in-house attorney to make sure that all laws are being adhered to when stating a policy.

  - Guidelines for maintaining a safe work environment - whether you are on a construction job site or sitting in an office this section applies. Maintaining a safe work environment is not only a legal requirement but also one that will promote employee engagement. Failure to do so could expose the company to legal liability and potential regulatory scrutiny.

- <u>Communication and Transparency</u>

  - Standards for communication within the organization and with external stakeholders - having some level of control over what is being said is important. The expectations here are that an employee will not openly talk to the press or an external party without first discussing it with the company. Making sure that inquiries are distributed to the right person within the company is vital to protecting the reputation and brand. Also important is that you do not discourage employees from filing whistleblower claims. Whistleblower laws exist globally, and employers are generally not permitted to prohibit employees from making claims.

  - Expectations regarding honesty and transparency in all dealings - while this seems innate to any organization, there is a reason it is listed here: to protect the organization if an employee is determined to have acted in contravention of these principles.

- <u>Accountability and Enforcement</u>

  - Procedures for reporting unethical behavior or policy violations - this should include not only whistleblower policies of compliance with SOX but also describe the chain of command (e.g. does an employee go to their manager first or HR or compliance). This is an important fundamental for rooting out and identifying bad behavior within an organization.

  - Description of the process for investigating complaints - the detail here should not be too descriptive and should live in another policy but it should give transparency to employees about the process and their expectations. For example, it should cover the timing of investigations, prohibitions on retaliation and whether a response will be provided to the complainant.

- Consequences of violating the Code of Conduct - a must for any code of conduct. This should be clear and detail the consequences for violating the code. Many codes have language that states "…up to and including termination." make sure to get buy in from senior leaders and HR prior to including such language.

- Implementation and Oversight

  - Roles and responsibilities in enforcing the Code of Conduct - informing employees, managers, and supervisors of their responsibilities in the code is essential. Without knowing what is required, violations or potential acts of fraud could be occurring.

  - Training and resources available to help employees adhere to the code - this will be discussed later in the chapter, but training on the code is required for any employee. Without proper training, employees would be unaware of what is required of them.

  - Regular review and updating of the code - the code is not a static document and should be formally reviewed and adopted at least once a year. This includes socializing the draft with all relevant stakeholders to ensure their buy-in of the requirements and making needed changes based on various factors.

- Conclusion

  - Affirmation of the importance of the Code of Conduct - annually all of those subject to the code should be signing off on their compliance. This provides a record for the organization that all employees, or others, have been trained and affirmed their compliance with the code.

- Encouragement for all members to uphold the standards set forth in the document

A good code of conduct helps guide an organization. As previously noted, try making it as easy of a read as possible. Many organizations publish their code or post it on their website. I would encourage you to look at other codes and see what aspects you admire.

ii) Policy

Policies are specific guidelines that dictate how certain aspects of business should be conducted. They provide clear instructions and boundaries for acceptable behavior and practices.

Some common examples of policies include:

- **Data Protection Policies**: In the digital age, protecting personal information is paramount. Compliance with data protection laws like the General Data Protection Regulation (GDPR) in the EU or similar regulations worldwide ensures that customer information is handled securely and privacy is maintained. For example, a company might implement policies that dictate how employee and customer data are stored, accessed, and shared.

- **Workplace Safety Policies**: Compliance with occupational safety and health regulations is crucial for protecting employees. In the United States, the Occupational Safety and Health Administration (OSHA) mandates standards that include proper training, equipment, and emergency procedures to minimize workplace injuries and hazards.

- **Anti-discrimination Policies**: These policies are vital for fostering an inclusive work environment. They ensure that all employees have equal access to opportunities and are free from harassment and discrimination based on race, gender, age, religion, or other protected characteristics. An example is a policy that outlines the procedures for handling complaints about workplace harassment, ensuring they are investigated fairly and promptly.

- **Insider Trading Policies:** These policies outline who has access to what sensitive data and prohibit using sensitive data to profit from personal trading habits. These ensure that the organization takes the laws governing insider trading seriously and prohibits employees from taking certain actions. They may also list prohibitions from accessing certain information or creating "blackout" periods on trading for those who may have insider information.

Reviewing and updating compliance policies is an essential process for any organization striving to stay aligned with evolving laws, technological advancements, and shifting business goals. This ongoing task ensures that policies not only meet current legal requirements but also support efficient and responsible business practices. Here's an in-depth look at the key steps involved in maintaining the relevance of compliance policies:

1. Regular Review Schedules

Organizations should establish regular intervals for reviewing compliance policies. Typically, this could be annually or bi-annually but may vary depending on the industry's dynamic nature or regulatory environment. For example, the tech industry faces frequent changes in data protection laws and would benefit from more frequent reviews. Setting a fixed schedule ensures that no aspect of compliance becomes outdated and that all policies reflect the latest legal and ethical standards.

## 2. Monitoring Changes in Legal Requirements

A critical component of the review process is staying informed about changes in relevant laws and regulations. This requires a proactive approach, possibly involving a dedicated legal or compliance team that monitors regulatory updates. Tools such as legal databases, newsletters from regulatory bodies, and memberships in professional compliance organizations can be invaluable. These resources help organizations anticipate changes and adapt their policies accordingly.

## 4. Alignment with Business Objectives

As business objectives evolve, so must compliance policies. For example, if a company plans to expand into new markets, its compliance framework must be assessed to ensure it covers international trade laws or foreign regulatory requirements. Strategic business reviews should include a compliance aspect, ensuring that policies support rather than hinder business growth and adaptation.

## 5. Stakeholder Engagement

Involving various stakeholders in the review process is crucial for comprehensive policy updates. This includes gathering input from department heads, legal counsel, HR, and even frontline employees who are directly affected by certain policies. Such collaboration can highlight practical challenges and operational insights that might not be evident from a top-down perspective.

## 6. Training and Communication

Once policies are updated, effectively communicating these changes to all employees is vital for compliance. Regular training sessions, updated manuals, and digital resources ensure that the workforce is informed and compliant. Additionally, feedback mechanisms should be established so employees can report on the practicality of new policies and suggest further improvements.

iii) Procedure

A procedure is a prescribed way of undertaking a process or a part of a process, encompassing a sequence of steps to be executed in a particular order to achieve a desired result. While closely related, procedures differ from policies; policies provide the overarching guidelines and rules within which an organization operates, and procedures detail the specific methods of implementing those policies.

Definition and Role of Procedures

Procedures are essential in any organizational setup, providing a standardized method to carry out activities consistently and efficiently. By defining clear procedures, organizations ensure that tasks are completed correctly and uniformly, reducing variability and enhancing reliability in outcomes. Procedures typically include information such as the purpose of the process, the scope of where and when it applies, step-by-step instructions to follow, and the roles and responsibilities of those involved.

Interdependencies with Policies

Procedures and policies are interdependent, supporting organizational governance by ensuring that the workforce operates within defined boundaries and towards common objectives. Policies set the direction and the rules, while procedures provide the practical steps needed to enact those policies. This relationship can be seen as hierarchical:

policies are the governing principles, and procedures are the operational actions derived from these principles.

For example, a company might have a policy that requires maintaining confidentiality of client data. The procedure to support this policy would detail the specific steps employees must take when handling such data, including how to securely store files, how to share them safely with authorized personnel, and how to dispose of documents containing sensitive information.

Examples of Procedures

Procedures can vary widely depending on the specific needs of an organization and the sector in which it operates. Here are a few examples illustrating how procedures are applied in different contexts:

1. Emergency Evacuation Procedures: In a manufacturing plant, the safety policy dictates that the health and safety of employees must be protected. The emergency evacuation procedure supports this policy by providing detailed instructions on what employees should do in the event of a fire or other emergency. This might include steps like sounding the alarm, calling emergency services, and using designated evacuation routes.

2. Customer Complaint Handling Procedures: A retail company may have a policy aimed at ensuring customer satisfaction. The corresponding procedure would outline the steps for handling customer complaints, from the initial customer contact all the way through to resolution. These steps could include logging the complaint, investigating the issue, communicating with the customer throughout the process, and providing a resolution or compensation if necessary.

3. Hiring Procedures: An HR policy could stipulate the company's commitment to equal opportunity and non-discrimination in hiring. The hiring procedure that enforces this policy would include steps for posting job ads, screening applicants, conducting interviews, and selecting candidates, all designed to eliminate bias and promote fairness.

4. Financial Auditing Procedures: To comply with a financial management policy, an organization might implement a procedure for regular audits. This procedure would specify how and when audits are to be conducted, who will conduct them, how discrepancies should be reported, and how audit results are to be documented and reviewed.

Each example demonstrates how procedures operationalize policies, providing a clear roadmap for individuals within the organization to follow, thereby ensuring compliance, efficiency, and consistency in activities. This structural relationship between policies and procedures not only supports operational success but also helps in achieving strategic objectives by aligning day-to-day operations with the broader goals of the organization. By effectively linking policies with practical procedures, organizations can foster a disciplined and systematic approach to business management and document compliance with relevant rules and regulations.


iv) Manual/Handbook

Compliance manuals serve as vital tools in any organization, encapsulating the specific practices, responsibilities, and standards required to adhere to applicable laws, regulations, and company policies. These manuals are integral to maintaining legal and ethical integrity across an organization's operations, providing a clear guide for employees at all levels.

Purpose and Contents of Compliance Manuals

The primary purpose of a compliance manual is to compile all the compliance-related information in a single, accessible document that helps ensure all members of an organization understand and can implement compliance requirements effectively. A well-structured compliance manual typically includes:

- Introduction: Explains the scope and purpose of the manual, including who must adhere to it.

- Compliance Policies: Details the organization's policy statements regarding compliance with specific laws and regulations relevant to the business.

- Procedures: Outlines specific procedures for compliance-related tasks, including reporting mechanisms, auditing procedures, and corrective actions.

- Roles and Responsibilities: Identifies the compliance roles within the organization, detailing the responsibilities of each role, from the compliance officer to the department heads and general staff.

- Risk Management Strategies: Discusses how to identify, assess, and mitigate compliance risks.

- Emergency Contacts and Resources: Provides contact information for key personnel and external resources in case of compliance queries or issues.

Benefits of Using Compliance Manuals

The use of compliance manuals brings numerous benefits to an organization:

1. Consistency: By having a single, comprehensive source of compliance information, organizations ensure consistent adherence to required standards across all departments and locations, minimizing errors and discrepancies.

2. Efficiency: Employees save time and resources by referring to a well-documented manual that provides clear guidelines and instructions for compliance-related tasks, thereby streamlining processes.

3. Training and Onboarding: Compliance manuals are crucial in training new employees, helping them understand their compliance obligations from the start. They also serve as a reference tool for ongoing employee education.

4. Legal Safeguarding: In the event of legal scrutiny, a well-maintained compliance manual can demonstrate an organization's commitment to regulatory compliance, potentially mitigating penalties.

Examples of Compliance Manual Use:

- In the financial sector, a bank's compliance manual includes detailed procedures for customer due diligence and anti-money laundering protocols. This helps ensure all employees follow the same steps in vetting new clients and reporting suspicious activities.

- A pharmaceutical company uses its compliance manual to guide staff through the complex regulatory environment, ensuring adherence to FDA regulations concerning drug trials, marketing, and patient safety.

Maintenance and Accessibility of Compliance Manuals

Regular Updates: Compliance manuals must be regularly updated to reflect changes in laws and regulations, technological advancements, and shifts in business operations. This typically involves a scheduled review process, either annually or biannually, and ad hoc updates when significant regulatory changes occur.

Accessibility: Ensuring that the compliance manual is easily accessible to all employees is crucial. This often means making the manual available both in print and digitally, such as on the company intranet or through specialized compliance software that allows for easy updates and access.

Feedback Mechanisms: Incorporating a system for feedback on the manual's usefulness and clarity can help improve its effectiveness. Employees should have the means to report any ambiguities or suggest enhancements based on their practical experiences.

Compliance manuals are not merely administrative documents; they are dynamic tools that play a critical role in the operational and ethical framework of an organization. They ensure that all employees are equipped to uphold and act in accordance with both internal and external compliance requirements, thereby safeguarding the organization against risks and contributing to its overall success and integrity.

## Writing Compliance Policies and Procedures

Writing effective compliance policies and procedures is critical for any organization, particularly in highly regulated industries like financial services. These documents serve as the foundation for ensuring that an organization adheres to regulatory standards and operates with integrity. This guide will explore the fundamental building blocks of writing compliance policies and procedures, embedding the key elements of "who, what, where, why, when, and how documented" into each section, with some specific examples from the financial industry.

Part of the "why" of these documents is, of course, to minimize risk and protect the organization from fines and penalties associated with non-compliance. They also play a crucial role in maintaining the organization's reputation with clients and the public.

<u>Writing Compliance Policies</u>

As discussed above, policies and procedures differ in nature. Policies tend to be more concise and are limited to explaining the requirements and expectations placed on people or processes. That being said, they should be written using the same principles of "what, who, where, why, when, and how documented" described below.

What: Compliance policies are broad statements of principles that guide an organization's decision-making and behavior concerning regulatory and legal obligations. What should define the purpose of the policy and its stated objective?

Who: These are generally developed by a compliance team with input from senior management to ensure alignment with organizational goals and legal requirements. The "Who" deals with who the policies apply to. Is it employees, vendors, contractors, interns? Policies vary in application for many reasons, so being specific is key.

Where: The policies could apply across the organization, in all departments and locations where the organization operates. Or the policy could be local or business-specific. Aside from the Who, this is important for individuals to be aware if certain policies that exist in different jurisdictions.

Why: The purpose is to establish a culture of compliance and integrity, providing a framework for consistent decision-making. There may also be legal or regulatory standards. Point these out in the policy cite the specific rule or statute. This will give the policy credibility.

When: The When could mean the applicability of a policy, such as a certain new policy or new changes taking place in a fiscal year. It could also apply to certain processes or behaviors. For example, when traveling abroad for business or when entertaining clients.

How documented: Explain in detail how compliance with this policy is documented. Is it by attestation, training, or recording certain events? Be specific here. This is also helpful when explaining the policy to regulators or auditors.

Example: A bank might have a compliance policy that outlines the principles for anti-money laundering (AML), stating its commitment to preventing any transactions that facilitate money laundering or the funding of terrorist activities (*What*). This policy applies to all employees who facilitate customer bank transactions (*Who*) in the United States (*Where*). The policy is being enacted due to the USA PATRIOT ACT and other various AML requirements (Why). All client transactions affected on a monthly basis should be screened for AML requirements (*When*). The organizations AML System conducts the screening and identifies potential red flags (*How documented*).

<u>Writing Compliance Procedures</u>

Compliance procedures are detailed, step-by-step instructions that outline how to implement the policies. These tend to be much more detailed and may also be referred to as Standard Operating Procedures (SOPs). These are helpful because they tie back to policy requirements, which then tie back to the risk assessment. What is important in any procedure or SOP is that a detailed outline of the control points is described.

What: This should be a general overview of what the procedure is attempting to accomplish.

Who: This is different from a policy because it should cover who is responsible for the process being addressed. This can be a person's title or actual name. Given the turnover that occurs in industries, it is probably recommended to put a specific title or function as opposed to a name.

Where: These apply in specific operational contexts where detailed guidance is needed to comply with policies.

Why: Procedures are critical for ensuring that the policy's intentions are effectively translated into actionable and consistent practices across the organization. Explaining the why helps tie it back to a specific policy or regulation and is beneficial for external parties and employees performing the function.

When: Is this a daily process? Weekly? Monthly? Annually? Describe in detail in this section when the procedure is taking place. Not all processes are the same, so be specific here.

How documented: The record keeping of the process is essential. Knowing where certain records are stored and in which format is key to any procedure.

Example: Following the AML policy, a financial services firm might have procedures that include customer due diligence processes, such as verifying customer identity, understanding the nature of the customer's activities, and assessing money laundering risks associated with that customer.

<u>Anti-Money Laundering (AML) Compliance Procedure: Customer Due Diligence</u>

1. What: Customer Due Diligence Process

This procedure outlines the steps necessary for conducting due diligence on new and existing customers to prevent and detect money laundering activities. It is designed to verify the identity of customers, understand the nature of their activities, and assess the risks associated with their transactions.

2. Who's Responsible

- Compliance Officer: Oversees the AML compliance program, ensures the procedure is up-to-date and in line with regulations, and handles reporting to authorities.

- Customer Service Representatives (CSRs): Conduct initial customer identification and document collection.

- Risk Management Team: Assesses risk level based on the collected data and ongoing monitoring.

3. Where

This procedure is applied in all branches and offices of the financial institution, as well as through any online platforms where customer interactions or transactions occur.

4. Why

The customer due diligence process is a critical component of the institution's AML compliance efforts per the USA PATRIOT Act and Bank Secrecy Act. It helps to:

- Identify and verify the identity of customers to ensure they are who they claim to be.

- Understand the customer's business and transaction patterns to identify any activities that deviate from normal expected activities, which might suggest money laundering.

- Comply with national and international regulations regarding AML practices, thus avoiding potential fines and legal penalties.

## 5. When

- At Account Opening: Customer due diligence must be performed before opening any new accounts.

- During Ongoing Relationships: Regular reviews are conducted based on the risk profile; for high-risk customers, reviews are annual, and for low-risk customers, less frequently at least every 2 years.

- Upon Detection of Suspicious Activity: If unusual patterns are detected during routine monitoring, additional due diligence is triggered.

## 6. How Documented

Step 1: Identification and Verification

- Collect legally acceptable identification documents (e.g., passport, driver's license).

- Verify the authenticity of documents through an in-person check or certified digital verification tools.

- Record and store all identification information in the customer's compliance file.

Step 2: Understanding Customer Activities

- Obtain information about the nature of the customer's business through a questionnaire filled out during the account opening.

- Use public and private databases to corroborate the information provided.

- Document the expected nature and volume of transactions.

Step 3: Risk Assessment

- Classify customers into risk categories (low, medium, high) based on factors such as country of origin, business type, transaction volume, and transaction types.

- Document the rationale for risk categorization in the customer's compliance file.

Step 4: Monitoring and Reporting

- Implement transaction monitoring systems that flag transactions deviating from the customer's profile.

- Review and update customer information at predetermined intervals or when major changes in customer activity occur.

- Document any findings and actions taken in response to flagged transactions.

Step 5: Record Keeping

- Maintain all records related to customer due diligence for a minimum period as required by law (typically five years).

- Ensure all documentation is stored securely to protect customer privacy and comply with data protection regulations.

Example Compliance Documentation Entry:

Customer Name: John Doe

Account Number: 123456

Date of Onboarding: 2024-01-15

Documents Collected: Passport (No. XYZ123), Utility Bill dated 2024-01-10

Verification: In-person verification completed on 2024-01-15 by CSR Jane Smith

Risk Category: Medium (due to high transaction volume in international trade)

Monitoring Plan: Quarterly transaction review, annual comprehensive review

By following this detailed procedure, the financial institution ensures it not only complies with AML regulations but also plays a vital role in preventing financial crimes. As you can see a procedure is considerably longer in length and varies greatly from a policy. It gives precise step-by-step instructions and can be used by anyone performing the function.

## Separate Policies and Procedures vs. a Consolidated Manual

Below, I look at the pros and cons of having separate compliance policies and procedures versus a consolidated manual. This is a preference, not a requirement, and could be determined based on several factors: the complexity of the regulations to which you are subject, your organizations size, etc. Each approach has distinct advantages and disadvantages, affecting the organization's ability to implement and adhere to regulatory requirements effectively. Here, we explore the pros and cons of both methods to provide a clearer understanding of which approach might best suit an organization's needs.

<u>Separate Compliance Policies and Procedures</u>

Pros:

1. **Specialization and Focus**: Keeping policies and procedures separate allows each document to be highly specialized and focused. This can be particularly beneficial in complex regulatory environments where details matter. Separate documents ensure that specific procedures can be thoroughly detailed without being overshadowed by broad policy statements.

2. **Flexibility in Updates**: When policies and procedures are maintained separately, updating due to changes in law or operational practices can be more streamlined. If a change affects only the procedural aspect and not the underlying policy, only the relevant documents need to be revised, which can be less cumbersome and reduce the risk of inconsistencies.

3. **Targeted Training**: Separate documents can facilitate more targeted training programs. Employees who need to understand specific procedures can be trained without being overloaded with broad policy details that may not be directly relevant to their day-to-day responsibilities.

Cons:

1. **Complexity in Administration**: Managing a multitude of separate documents can become administratively burdensome. Ensuring that all employees have access to the correct, up-to-date version of each policy and procedure can be challenging, increasing the risk of non-compliance.

2. **Inconsistency Risks**: There is a higher risk of discrepancies or conflicts between policies and their corresponding procedures when they are documented separately. This can lead to confusion and errors in the application.

3. **Increased Training Requirements**: While targeted training is an advantage, it also means that comprehensive understanding across different areas may require multiple training sessions, which can be time-consuming and costly.

<u>Consolidated Compliance Manual</u>

Pros:

1. **Simplicity and Clarity**: A single compliance manual that integrates both policies and procedures provides a one-stop resource for employees. This integration can enhance clarity, making it easier for employees to understand how policies translate into specific actions.

2. **Consistency**: When policies and procedures are consolidated, it ensures alignment between the guiding principles and the actions required to fulfill them. This alignment can reduce misunderstandings and improve compliance adherence.

3. **Efficient Training and Updates**: Training employees become more straightforward with a consolidated manual, as there is just one document to disseminate and explain. Similarly, updates due to regulatory or operational changes can be managed more efficiently, as there's only one document to revise.

Cons:

1. **Overwhelming Information**: A comprehensive compliance manual can be quite extensive, potentially overwhelming users

with information. This can make it difficult for employees to find specific information relevant to their immediate needs.

2. **Slower Updates**: Updating a large, consolidated manual can be a slower process, especially if changes are extensive or affect several sections. This could delay the dissemination of new compliance information.

3. **Generic Detail Level**: To accommodate a wide range of topics, the details in a consolidated manual might be more generic than in specialized documents. This could potentially lead to gaps in understanding specific procedures or insufficient guidance on complex compliance issues.

The choice between separate documents and a consolidated manual depends on the organization's size, complexity, and specific regulatory environment. Larger organizations or those in highly regulated industries might benefit from the specialization afforded by separate documents, whereas smaller entities or those with less complex regulatory needs might prefer the simplicity of a consolidated manual. Ultimately, the decision should align with the organization's overall strategy for compliance, ensuring both practicality in day-to-day operations and adherence to regulatory requirements.

## Training

Some may ask, shouldn't training be its own separate fundamental? Why is it lumped together with policies? My answer would be that an effective compliance program has to train on all policies to increase awareness of what is expected and required. Training outside of policies and procedures is not a compliance function. There may be aspects of training in product, sales, HR, and other departments, and for that, compliance should give input but resist the urge to own that training. This next section will give a brief overview of the types of training. This is one faction of a compliance professional's job and good communication is key.

Compliance training is an essential component of an organization's risk management and ethics programs, ensuring that employees understand their compliance and ethical obligations and how to conduct themselves in various situations. It not only informs and educates employees about the laws, regulations, and company policy requirements pertinent to their specific roles but also reinforces the standards for behavior within the organization. The importance of compliance training extends across multiple dimensions, including legal liability, organizational integrity, and employee empowerment.

Reducing Liability

One of the primary reasons for implementing rigorous compliance training is to reduce liability for the organization. In highly regulated industries, such as finance, healthcare, and pharmaceuticals, failing to comply with laws and regulations can result in severe penalties, fines, and damages to reputation. Effective compliance training helps prevent such outcomes by making sure that employees know the regulatory requirements and understand the importance of adhering to them.

For example, in the healthcare sector, compliance training programs educate staff about patient privacy laws under HIPAA (Health Insurance Portability and Accountability Act). By understanding these regulations, healthcare professionals can make informed decisions about how to handle patient information, thereby avoiding potential legal issues that could arise from non-compliance.

Promoting Organizational Integrity and Trust

Compliance training plays a crucial role in building and maintaining integrity within the organization. It establishes a culture of honesty, responsibility, and ethical behavior that can enhance the trust and confidence of stakeholders, including customers, investors, and regulatory bodies. A company known for its commitment to compliance is more likely to be viewed favorably, which can be a significant competitive advantage.

In the financial industry, for instance, adherence to anti-money laundering (AML) regulations is crucial. Compliance training helps ensure that employees recognize suspicious activities and know how to report them appropriately. This not only helps prevent financial crimes but also boosts investor confidence by demonstrating the company's commitment to lawful and ethical business practices.

Enhancing Operational Effectiveness

Well-informed employees are more likely to perform their duties efficiently and make decisions that align with both legal standards and company policies. Compliance training equips employees with the knowledge to navigate complex regulatory environments without constant oversight, reducing the burden on compliance officers and allowing them to focus on more strategic issues like monitoring and testing, regulatory change management, etc.

Furthermore, compliance training can help standardize processes across the organization, ensuring consistency in how compliance issues are handled. This standardization can lead to operational efficiencies and a reduction in errors that might occur due to misunderstandings or misinterpretation of policies.

Employee Empowerment and Engagement

Effective compliance training empowers employees by providing them with the tools and knowledge they need to make the right decisions. This empowerment can lead to increased job satisfaction and engagement as employees feel more competent and secure in their roles. Moreover, it fosters an open workplace environment where employees feel confident to voice concerns and report wrongdoing without fear of retaliation.

Continuous Improvement and Adaptation

The regulatory landscape is constantly evolving, and compliance training must evolve with it to remain effective. Regularly updated training programs help organizations adapt to new laws and regulations, ensuring ongoing compliance and mitigating risks associated with regulatory changes.

For example, with the increasing focus on data protection and privacy, businesses globally must continually update their compliance training to cover new data protection laws like GDPR (General Data Protection Regulation) in the European Union or CCPA (California Consumer Privacy Act) in the United States.

## Types of training

Compliance training is a crucial aspect of an organization's operations, ensuring that employees are informed about the laws, regulations, and company policies relevant to their roles. The delivery of this training can be segmented into three primary types: in-person (live), online, and hybrid. Each method has its advantages and plays a vital role in comprehensive compliance education, adapting to various learning styles, and meeting logistical needs.

In-Person (Live) Training

In-person training involves live sessions typically conducted in a classroom setting or through workshops. This traditional form of training is highly interactive and allows for real-time feedback, discussions, and comprehensive engagement between trainers and participants. In-person training is particularly effective for complex subject matter where immediate clarification is needed, fostering a deeper understanding through personal interaction and live demonstrations.

The major advantage of in-person training is the opportunity for enhanced communication, which can lead to a more thorough comprehension of the compliance issues at hand. It also allows the trainer to adapt the session based on the audience's reactions and understanding, providing a personalized learning experience.

Online Training

Online training delivers compliance education through digital platforms (Learning Management Systems or LMS) and is accessible to participants regardless of their geographical locations. This method is highly scalable, making it easier and more cost-effective for organizations to train a large number of employees and ensure consistent delivery of training content.

A critical component of online training is the inclusion of quizzes to reinforce learning. Quizzes serve multiple educational functions: they test knowledge, reinforce learning by requiring trainees to recall information, and identify areas where participants may need additional help. The immediate feedback provided by online quizzes helps learners correct misunderstandings promptly, solidifying their understanding of the material. Furthermore, quizzes can increase engagement, as interactive elements help maintain the trainee's attention and make learning more enjoyable.

The use of quizzes also allows organizations to track completion and understanding of compliance topics, which is crucial for audit purposes and ensuring that all employees meet the necessary training requirements. This data can be invaluable for refining future training modules and identifying common areas of difficulty among employees.

Hybrid Training

Hybrid training combines elements of both in-person and online methodologies. This type of training might involve initial in-person sessions followed by online modules or vice versa. Hybrid approaches cater to different learning preferences and logistical needs, making training more accessible and flexible for employees.

The hybrid model can be particularly effective in compliance training because it allows for the breadth and consistent delivery of online learning while also providing the depth and interaction of in-person sessions. For instance, complex scenarios can be discussed and dissected in a live setting, while foundational knowledge and regulations can be reviewed through online modules.

Conclusion - Training

Each training method offers distinct advantages that can help an organization meet its compliance training needs effectively. In-person training is unmatched for its interactive potential and adaptability; online training offers unparalleled reach and consistency, enhanced significantly by the use of quizzes to ensure comprehension and engagement; and hybrid training provides a balanced approach that maximizes accessibility and effectiveness.

Ultimately, the choice of training method will depend on an organization's specific needs, the nature of the material to be covered, and the logistical realities of training a particular workforce.

However, in today's diverse and dispersed work environments, incorporating a mix of training types, particularly enhancing online training with quizzes, can provide comprehensive coverage and ensure that all employees are well-prepared to meet their compliance obligations.

## Conclusion

In conclusion, the importance of policies, procedures, and training on the requirements is fundamental to any compliance program. The policies derive from the risk assessment and the training is an essential control to document effectiveness. Effective compliance policies establish the framework within which an organization operates, setting out clear guidelines and expectations that ensure all business activities adhere to legal and ethical standards. These policies are born from thorough risk assessments that identify potential areas of vulnerability, allowing organizations to address these proactively.

Moreover, the role of training cannot be overstated. It acts not only as a method to inform and educate but as a vital tool for enforcing compliance and demonstrating the organization's commitment to regulatory adherence and ethical practices. Training equips employees with the necessary knowledge and skills to perform their duties within the legal boundaries and aligns their actions with the organization's core values and objectives.

Together, well-crafted policies and robust training programs form an integral part of the compliance architecture. They are both preventative and protective, reducing the likelihood of non-compliance and mitigating the consequences should breaches occur. This synergy not only enhances operational efficiency but also fortifies the organization's reputation, fostering trust among stakeholders and the public.

Thus, investing in comprehensive compliance policies and continuous training is not merely a regulatory obligation—it is a strategic imperative that significantly influences the sustainability and success of an organization. As regulatory landscapes continue to evolve and become more complex, the need for dynamic compliance programs becomes even more critical. Organizations that prioritize and continuously improve their compliance practices are better positioned to navigate these changes effectively and maintain a competitive edge in their respective industries. Therefore, it is essential for leaders to ensure that their compliance policies are up-to-date and that their training programs are engaging and effective, thereby securing their standing as responsible and reliable entities in the global market.

# Monitoring and Testing

Introduction to Compliance Monitoring and Testing

Central to every compliance program are two critical activities: compliance monitoring and compliance testing. This chapter aims to delve deep into these concepts, distinguishing between them, exploring their origins, and emphasizing their importance within a comprehensive compliance program.

Understanding Compliance Monitoring and Testing

"Compliance Monitoring" refers to the continuous and regular assessment processes that evaluate the effectiveness of an organization's compliance framework. This ongoing activity aims to ensure that the organization operates in alignment with internal and external compliance requirements. Monitoring is usually integrated into the day-to-day operations and is conducted by individuals within the organization who have compliance responsibilities. It includes regular reviews of operations, periodic audits by internal staff, and the tracking of compliance-related metrics.

"Compliance Testing", on the other hand, is more structured and specific in nature. It involves conducting specific tests to evaluate the effectiveness of an organization's internal controls, policies, and procedures against regulatory requirements. Compliance testing is typically periodic and may be conducted by external auditors or independent consultants. The testing process includes the detailed examination of processes, transactions, and controls to identify any gaps or deficiencies that might expose the organization to compliance risk.

The Nexus of Compliance Testing and Risk Assessment

The basis of what gets tested in compliance programs stems directly from the organization's compliance risk assessment, as discussed in the first chapter. A compliance risk assessment is a fundamental tool that helps identify the areas of highest risk to an organization from a regulatory compliance perspective. This assessment is dynamic and should be updated regularly to reflect changes in the regulatory landscape, business operations, or the occurrence of compliance incidents.

The outcomes of this risk assessment guide the focus of both compliance monitoring and testing activities. For instance, if a risk assessment identifies a high risk of non-compliance in data protection practices, the subsequent compliance tests might focus on evaluating the adequacy of encryption measures and access controls. This activity would likely happen on a more frequent basis than a risk that would be considered low. Similarly, monitoring activities might include frequent reviews of data handling practices across different departments.

Procedures and Control Testing

The specific controls tested during compliance testing are described in detail within the organization's procedures. These procedures outline the methodologies and processes for achieving compliance with applicable regulations and standards. They serve as a blueprint for both monitoring and testing, providing clear guidelines and criteria against which performance can be measured.

For example, a procedure might stipulate that all client data must be encrypted using specific technologies. Compliance testing would then involve a detailed examination of these encryption practices to ensure they are being implemented as per the procedure. Monitoring might involve regular checks to ensure that every new batch of client data undergoes encryption.

Importance of Monitoring and Testing in Compliance Programs

The importance of compliance monitoring and testing is paramount. These activities are crucial for the detection and mitigation of compliance risks. They help ensure that compliance procedures are not only followed but are effective and up to date with current laws and regulations.

Investing significant resources in compliance monitoring and testing is essential because these activities help prevent compliance failures that could result in hefty fines, legal challenges, and damage to an organization's reputation. Furthermore, they provide an organization with the confidence that it is operating ethically and in accordance with its values and legal obligations. In truth, these activities should be taking up a significant portion of the compliance program's activities. While risk assessments and policies/procedures are fundamental, they require a great deal of work upfront and then are refreshed as needed.  The compliance monitoring and testing activities are done on a much more frequent basis, sometimes daily. This can not be stressed enough when seeking resources for a compliance department.

Continuous Improvement and Compliance Excellence

Moreover, regular monitoring and testing foster a culture of continuous improvement within an organization. They provide critical feedback loops for management to understand the effectiveness of their compliance efforts and identify areas for enhancement. Through these activities, organizations can adapt more swiftly to new regulatory demands and internal challenges, enhancing their overall compliance posture and operational resilience.

Compliance monitoring and testing are not just regulatory requirements; they are vital practices that underpin the health and efficacy of an organization's compliance program. This chapter will further explore these concepts, their implementation, and their impact, providing readers with a comprehensive understanding of how to manage and excel in compliance efforts.

## Monitoring

There are many activities that could be considered monitoring, such as reviewing metrics associated with completion rates of required training across the organization. A compliance professional should review their daily activities to consider which of their duties fall into this role and make sure they are documenting their efforts. Creating a monitoring plan to evidence all of the areas in which this conduct occurs is essential to any compliance program. Not only does a monitoring plan assist in evidencing the controls being measured, it also evidences the extent of a compliance program's breadth of core duties.

Tracking and documenting results of compliance monitoring is also important in determining trends and patterns of non-compliance across an organization. This assists in identifying potential areas of concern but can also illustrate where risks have been mitigated or risks lowered. Sharing this information with senior management is key to showing the value a compliance department brings to an organization.

Below are some key areas to consider for your compliance monitoring program, along with examples of what that monitoring may look like. These are just examples; monitoring occurs in many different forms. Sometimes it is purely the collection of data from another department.

Other times it may consist of duties the compliance department itself performs.

## Regulatory Risk

"Regulatory risk" involves the threat that changes in laws and regulations will adversely affect an organization's operations, financial performance, or reputation. Compliance monitoring in this area ensures that the organization remains up-to-date with local, national, and international regulatory changes.

- Example: A pharmaceutical company must continuously monitor its compliance with the Food and Drug Administration (FDA) regulations concerning drug approvals, manufacturing processes, and marketing practices. This includes regular reviews of clinical trial protocols and adverse event reporting procedures to ensure that all activities comply with stringent regulatory standards. Documenting this process will allow the compliance department to be aware of events in the timeline, tracking the number of days to approvals, additional requests from regulators, and potential issues raised.

## Financial Risk

"Financial risk" relates to the possibility of financial losses due to failures in financial compliance, which could include errors in financial reporting, fraud, or non-compliance with tax laws.

- Example: A multinational corporation must monitor its adherence to the Sarbanes-Oxley Act, which mandates accurate financial reporting and the implementation of effective internal controls. Regular audits and reviews of financial statements and internal audit processes help ensure transparency and prevent financial discrepancies. Tracking the timing of filings or amendments to filings could help uncover breaks in control processes that assure accuracy.

## Privacy

"Privacy compliance" involves adhering to laws and regulations that protect individuals' personal information. This is increasingly significant in a world where data breaches can lead to significant financial penalties and loss of trust.

- Example: A tech company dealing with large volumes of personal data, such as user names, addresses, and payment information, must monitor compliance with the General Data Protection Regulation (GDPR) in the EU. This includes regular checks on data processing activities, data protection impact assessments, and the enforcement of user consent procedures. This may require compliance to collect data from the information security department of known or suspected breaches. Tracking this data along timelines may help uncover where significant upgrades are needed to software or jurisdictional anomalies.

Cybersecurity

"Cybersecurity compliance" ensures that an organization's information technology systems are secured against unauthorized access, attacks, or breaches, adhering to both regulatory and industry standards.

- Example: A financial institution must continually monitor its compliance with cybersecurity frameworks like the NIST Cybersecurity Framework. This involves periodic security assessments, penetration testing, and reviews of security incident response procedures. Making sure compliance is looped into these types of tests will help in tracking findings or issues uncovered and identify areas that may require upgrades to controls.

Ethics (Code of Conduct)

"Ethics and code of conduct compliance" focuses on monitoring adherence to organizational ethical standards and behavior guidelines. This is crucial for maintaining a corporate culture that upholds integrity and respect for legal and moral standards.

- Example: A corporation might regularly conduct surveys and reviews of employee behavior to ensure compliance with its code of conduct. Training sessions and internal communications could be monitored for alignment with ethical standards, particularly concerning issues like fraud. Compliance should monitor training completion rates and report to managers those individuals who have failed to complete training or completed it after the required deadline.

<u>Operations</u>

"Operational compliance" includes the systems and processes in place to ensure that all company operations are performed in accordance with industry standards and regulatory requirements.

- Example: A manufacturing company must monitor its compliance with health and safety regulations as well as environmental standards. Monitor the regular inspections and audits of operational procedures, safety protocols, and/or waste disposal practices to help ensure continuous compliance. Monitoring potential issues and violations to include data of location, department, and various other factors could assist in uncovering non-compliance or areas where more training is needed.

<u>Safety</u>

"Safety compliance" involves monitoring the adherence to safety standards and practices designed to protect the health and well-being of employees and the public.

- Example: In industries such as construction or chemical manufacturing, regular safety audits and incident reporting are essential. Monitoring might include checks on the use of personal protective equipment (PPE), adherence to safety training procedures, and compliance with OSHA regulations.

<u>Conflicts of Interest</u>

"Conflicts of interest compliance" ensures that employees and management avoid situations where personal interests could interfere with their duties to the organization.

- Example: A compliance department may monitor for conflicts of interest by reviewing new client engagements and continuously updating its internal conflict-of-interest policies. This includes training sessions to educate employees on identifying and reporting potential conflicts. Having employees report on personal investments or outside business activities could assist in finding instances where an employee may be conflicted.

Effective compliance monitoring spans a broad spectrum of operational areas within an organization, each critical to maintaining the legal and ethical standards necessary for successful operation. By rigorously applying compliance monitoring practices in these key areas, organizations can not only avoid the consequences of non-compliance but also enhance their operational integrity and trustworthiness. This continuous vigilance fosters a culture of compliance that permeates every level of the organization, supporting its long-term stability and growth.

## Frequency of Monitoring

The frequency at which compliance monitoring activities are conducted is not arbitrary; rather, it is intricately linked to the outcome of compliance risk assessments, particularly the residual risk. This discussion will delve into how residual risk informs the frequency of compliance monitoring, ensuring that resources are allocated effectively and risks are managed efficiently.

Understanding Residual Risk in Compliance Risk Assessments

As discussed in the first chapter, residual risk is the risk that remains after all control measures and mitigation strategies have been applied to an inherent risk. It is essentially the level of risk an organization is willing to accept after implementing its risk response strategy. Compliance risk assessments aim to identify and prioritize risks based on their potential impact and the likelihood of occurrence. Once these risks are identified, control measures are put in place to mitigate them to acceptable levels, which is where the concept of residual risk comes into play.

The assessment of residual risk is critical because it determines not only the nature of the controls needed but also the intensity and frequency of monitoring required to ensure those controls are effective and continue to operate as intended.

Linking Residual Risk to Compliance Monitoring Frequency

The direct linkage between residual risk and the frequency of compliance monitoring is grounded in the principle of proportionality: higher risks require more frequent monitoring, while lower risks might justify less frequent checks. This approach ensures that monitoring efforts are both efficient and effective, focusing resources where they are most needed.

1. "High Residual Risk Areas": Areas where the residual risk is deemed high are typically those where the potential impact of non-compliance is severe or where the likelihood of non-compliance is high. In such cases, frequent and comprehensive monitoring is necessary. This might include weekly or monthly reviews and audits to ensure that the control measures are effectively managing the risk.

- Example: If a financial institution identifies a high residual risk in its anti-money laundering (AML) controls, due to the fast-changing nature of regulatory requirements, it would likely increase the frequency of its monitoring activities. This could involve more frequent staff training, closer scrutiny of transaction reports, and regular updates to compliance protocols to align with the latest regulatory guidance.

2. Moderate Residual Risk Areas: For risks classified as moderate, monitoring activities do not need to be as frequent as those for high-risk areas but should still be regular enough to ensure that the risk remains controlled. Quarterly or bi-annual reviews might be sufficient.

- Example: A manufacturing company might find a moderate residual risk in its environmental compliance due to previous successful mitigations. Periodic monitoring might then focus on ensuring that waste management procedures are followed and that new regulations are integrated into company practices.

3. Low Residual Risk Areas: In areas where the residual risk is low, less frequent monitoring might be justified. However, it is crucial that these areas are not ignored entirely, as non-compliance can still occur, potentially elevating the risk over time. Annual reviews might be appropriate in such cases.

- Example: For a technology company that has robust and proven cybersecurity measures in place, with a history of no breaches and low risk of data theft, the residual risk may be considered low. Annual compliance checks and system reviews might suffice to ensure systems are secure and protections are current.

Adaptive Compliance Monitoring

The relationship between residual risk and the frequency of compliance monitoring highlights the need for an adaptive compliance monitoring strategy. As the risk landscape evolves—whether due to changes in the business environment, regulatory amendments, or the outcome of previous monitoring activities—the assessment of residual risks should be revisited and monitoring frequencies adjusted accordingly. These outcomes of the monitoring activity should be considered when reassessing your risk assessment. Areas that were previously considered low but have high rates of findings may indicate that the control effectiveness is not measure appropriately. For example a control previously rated as effective could not withstand that scrutiny if there are a high level of findings.

This adaptive approach not only maximizes resource efficiency but also enhances the responsiveness of the compliance function to emerging risks. Organizations must maintain dynamic risk assessment processes with a clear mechanism to recalibrate monitoring frequencies based on the latest residual risk evaluations.

The frequency of compliance monitoring is intricately and necessarily tied to the residual risk determined in compliance risk assessments. By calibrating monitoring activities to the level of residual risk, organizations can ensure that their compliance efforts are both proportionate to the risks they face and effective in mitigating those risks. This strategy not only prevents compliance failures and reduces the likelihood of regulatory penalties but also supports a culture of compliance that permeates throughout the organization, enhancing overall governance and stability.

## Using Tools for Compliance Monitoring

The use of specialized tools in a compliance monitoring program is paramount to the effectiveness and efficiency of ensuring that an organization adheres to regulatory standards and internal policies. Tools such as Microsoft Excel and Power BI offer capabilities that greatly enhance the ability to collect, analyze, and report data related to compliance activities. These tools can automate routine data processing tasks, thereby reducing the likelihood of human error and increasing the accuracy of the compliance reports. For instance, Excel can be used to track compliance data across various departments, consolidate information into centralized reports, and perform basic data analysis, such as identifying compliance rates and non-compliance issues.

Further leveraging advanced tools like Power BI transforms how organizations handle data by enabling more sophisticated data visualization and analytics. Power BI allows compliance officers to create dynamic dashboards that provide real-time insights into compliance data. This capability is invaluable for identifying trends and patterns that may not be apparent from raw data alone. For example, Power BI can visualize trends in compliance failures across different regions or departments, helping to pinpoint systemic issues or areas requiring additional focus. Tracking these findings over time supports the development of a proactive compliance strategy, where potential issues can be addressed before they escalate into significant problems. If you are unfamiliar with Power BI, there are plenty of free resources available on the internet. I would recommend becoming familiar with this tool or ones similar (like Tableau) as the analysis of data is key to any compliance monitoring program.

Moreover, the use of these tools in a compliance monitoring program not only enhances the immediate analysis of compliance data but also aids in long-term strategic planning. By maintaining historical compliance data and tracking the outcomes of compliance activities over time, organizations can identify long-term trends and assess the effectiveness of their compliance policies and procedures. This historical insight is crucial for the continuous improvement of the compliance program, as it allows for the adjustment of strategies based on proven data and trends. Additionally, such tools support regulatory audits by providing auditors with clear, well-organized data, thereby facilitating a smoother audit process. Overall, incorporating tools like Excel and Power BI into compliance monitoring is essential for modern compliance management, offering both strategic depth and operational efficiency.

## Testing

Compliance testing plays a crucial role in an organization's overall compliance framework, serving as a more specific and targeted approach to ensuring that specific company operations adhere to legal, regulatory, and ethical standards. Unlike compliance monitoring, which is continuous and integrated into daily operations, compliance testing is periodic and conducted at specific intervals to provide an in-depth examination of the company's compliance with its policies and the regulatory requirements that govern its industry. This targeted approach allows for a detailed assessment of how well the internal controls are working and whether they are effective in mitigating compliance risks.

The specificity of compliance testing is what sets it apart from broader compliance monitoring efforts. While monitoring might include general reviews and observations of ongoing activities, compliance testing involves systematic tests designed to challenge the existing control framework and identify vulnerabilities. For instance, in a financial institution, compliance testing might involve detailed audits of transaction records to identify any breaches of anti-money laundering regulations. This kind of precise, focused scrutiny ensures that the organization can trust its framework to protect it from compliance failures and the resulting legal and reputational consequences.

The importance of compliance testing extends beyond mere adherence to regulations; it is fundamental to maintaining an organization's integrity and public trust. By conducting thorough and specific compliance tests, organizations can uncover potential weaknesses in their compliance strategies before they lead to serious issues. This proactive approach not only helps in aligning with current regulations but also prepares the organization for future changes in the regulatory environment. Compliance testing thus becomes an essential component of a robust risk management strategy, safeguarding the organization against potential fines, penalties, and damage to its reputation.

The formulation of a compliance testing plan should be done every year after the risk assessment is updated. This should be done by developing a plan and determining resources needed to execute the plan. Pay close attention to all risk areas identified by the risk assessment and do not just test "high" risk areas. Formulating and socializing the plan will also assist in determining which areas will be covered and whether gaps exist. Have this plan in place and begin execution at the beginning of each year while allowing for flexibility in case things change, in which they certainly will. It does not have to be set in stone, but it also shows regulators and other external parties that you take your compliance testing program seriously.

This chapter will delve into the many different facets of compliance testing, including scoping, re-performance versus outcome, sampling, exceptions, and drafting/publishing reports. Compliance testing is more science than art. It requires careful planning to ensure controls are being properly tested. This part of the compliance program should be taken very seriously as findings could have consequences that could include uncovering non-compliance or potential violations of law. It is best of the compliance testing program is handled as a "full-time job" by a member of the compliance department. However, those compliance professionals who are a department of one should take this aspect of their duties seriously and spend a considerable amount of time conducting compliance testing on the controls on which they rely.

## Scoping a Compliance Test

Scoping is a critical first step in the process of compliance testing, serving as the foundation upon which effective and efficient testing is built. Proper scoping ensures that the compliance test is targeted and relevant, focusing on the specific areas that present the highest risk or are most critical to the organization's compliance efforts. By defining the scope of a compliance test, an organization can allocate resources appropriately, focusing time and expertise on the areas that matter most. This targeted approach not only enhances the effectiveness of the compliance program by ensuring that critical controls are thoroughly tested, but also maximizes resource utilization, preventing the wastage of valuable time and effort on low-risk or irrelevant areas.

Researching the specific control being tested is an essential part of the scoping process. This involves a deep understanding of the control's purpose, the regulatory or internal requirements it addresses, and the risks it mitigates. Familiarity with the relevant documents and data that exist is crucial because it informs the tester about what exactly needs to be evaluated and how best to approach the evaluation. For instance, knowing which documents, such as policies, procedures, or previous audit reports, are relevant to the control being tested can provide insights into how the control has been designed and how it has performed historically. This knowledge is vital for crafting effective test plans that accurately assess whether the control is functioning as intended.

Moreover, an in-depth understanding of the available documents and data facilitates a more streamlined and effective testing process. When testers are well-prepared with the right documentation and data, they can conduct their assessments more efficiently and with greater precision. This preparation allows them to quickly identify any deviations from expected control operations and to understand the implications of these deviations on the organization's compliance posture. Additionally, having a thorough grasp of the data associated with the control, such as performance metrics or compliance rates, enables testers to perform detailed analyses to uncover underlying issues or trends that may not be apparent from a superficial review. Therefore, the importance of scoping and research in compliance testing cannot be overstated, as these steps critically determine the success and thoroughness of the compliance evaluation process.

Conducting interviews of all individuals in the process of being tested should also be done for two key reasons. First, to understand the actual timeline of the process, where control points exist, and the documents or data created and maintained. Second, give advanced notice that testing will be undertaken. While this may seem inconsistent with the norms of alerting someone, you will be scrutinizing their process because they could seek to conceal unethical behavior. It rarely works that way. While "surprise" tests have their place in a compliance program, they often cause frustration and distrust if performed across the board. Remember, the department, process or control being tested has specific duties they need to perform as part of the organization. A compliance test can be disruptive as it would take time away from regular day-to-day activities and require the production of documents or data.

## Testing Scripts

In the scoping of a test, the development of a testing script is paramount. This will serve to document the activities tested versus the subsequent controls. Let's dive into an example of creating a testing script for Anti-Money Laundering (AML).

Step 1: Define the Scope and Objective of the Test

The first step in creating a compliance testing script is to define its scope and objectives clearly. For AML compliance, this means identifying the specific processes, accounts, or transactions that will be examined. The objective might be to verify the effectiveness of the institution's customer due diligence processes, transaction monitoring systems, or compliance with reporting obligations.

Step 2: Identify Relevant AML Controls

Once the scope and objectives are set, the next step is to identify the AML controls that apply to the areas being tested. These controls could include customer identity verification procedures, systems for monitoring suspicious activities, or processes for filing Suspicious Activity Reports (SARs). Each control should be well-documented, with clear criteria for what constitutes compliance.

Step 3: Develop Test Steps

Develop specific test steps for each identified control. These steps should be actionable and measurable. For instance, if testing the control related to customer identity verification, steps might include reviewing a sample of new customer accounts to ensure that identification documents were collected and verified according to policy.

Step 4: Define Success Criteria

For each test step, define what success looks like. Success criteria should be directly linked to the regulatory requirements and the institution's internal policies. These criteria will serve as the benchmarks against which actual practices are evaluated.

Step 5: Execute the Test

Execute the test according to the script. This involves gathering data, interviewing staff, and reviewing documents and records. It's crucial to document each step taken and the findings from each test.

Example: Testing a Customer Account Opening Form

Let's consider a practical example where a bank's Customer Account Opening Form is tested against three different AML controls:

1. Control 1: Customer Identification Program (CIP)

   - Objective: To verify that the form collects all necessary information to confirm the identity of new customers.

   - Test Steps:

   - Review a sample of completed Customer Account Opening Forms.

   - Check that each form includes the customer's name, date of birth, address, and identification number (e.g., Social Security number).

   - Success Criteria:

   - 100% of the forms should have complete and accurate identity information.

2. Control 2: Due Diligence for Politically Exposed Persons (PEPs)

   - Objective: To ensure that the form includes a section for identifying whether the customer is a politically exposed person.

- Test Steps:

- Review the same sample of forms to check for a question regarding the PEP status of the customer.

- Verify if additional due diligence was performed for customers identified as PEPs.

- Success Criteria:

- All forms should include a PEP declaration section.

- There should be evidence of enhanced due diligence for customers declared as PEPs.

3. Control 3: CIP Risk Assessment Compatibility

- Objective: To assess whether the form facilitates a risk-based approach to customer acceptance.

- Test Steps:

- Review the forms to ensure they include questions about the customer's occupation, source of funds, and intended account usage.

- Determine if the responses influence the risk profile assigned to each customer.

- Success Criteria:

- The form should allow for the collection of sufficient information to assess the customer's risk level.

- The risk level should be clearly indicated on the form and influence monitoring intensity.

| Control ID | Control Description | Objective of Test | Test Steps | Success Criteria | Sample Data Reviewed | Findings |
|---|---|---|---|---|---|---|
| CIP001 | Customer Identification | Verify identity information is complete | Review 20 account opening forms | 100% of forms should have complete information | Form IDs 001-020 | All forms completed |
| PEP001 | PEP Screening | Ensure PEP status is checked | Check forms for PEP question, review responses | All forms should include a PEP section | Form IDs 021-040 | 2 forms missing PEP section |
| RISK001 | Risk Assessment | Assess risk-based approach to customer acceptance | Review forms for risk-related questions | Forms should assess customer's risk level | Form IDs 041-060 | Risk levels appropriately assigned |

Here is an example of creating a detailed compliance testing script for the control identified as CIP001, which involves Customer Identification Program (CIP) compliance and requires a structured approach to ensure that all aspects of the control are thoroughly evaluated. Below, I outline a comprehensive testing script that can be utilized in a spreadsheet or database format to conduct effective testing.

Compliance Testing Script for CIP001: Customer Identification

Control ID: CIP001

Control Description: Customer Identification

Objective of Test: To verify that identity information for new customers is complete and accurate as per regulatory requirements.

1. Preparation Phase:

   - Define Scope: Review new customer accounts opened within the last quarter.

   - Select Sample: Randomly select a sample of 20 customer accounts from the new accounts opened.

   - Gather Documentation: Collect all relevant forms and supporting documents for each selected account, including account opening forms, identity verification documents, and system logs showing the verification process.

2. Testing Steps:

   - Step 1: Review each selected account opening form to ensure all required fields related to customer identity are fully completed. These fields typically include the customer's full name, date of birth, address, and identification number (e.g., social security number, passport number).

   - Step 2: Verify that copies of identity verification documents (e.g., driver's license, passport) are attached to each customer's record and that the document details match the information provided in the account opening form.

- Step 3: Check system logs to confirm that each identity document was verified against a reliable, independent source (e.g., credit bureau, government database) at the time of account creation.

- Step 4: Assess any discrepancies or missing information and note the potential reasons (e.g., system error, human error).

3. Success Criteria:

- All reviewed account opening forms must have 100% completion of identity-related fields.

- Document attachments must be present for all accounts and must match the account information.

- System logs must show a verification check against an independent source for 100% of the cases.

4. Documentation:

- Data Entry: For each account in the sample, enter findings into the testing script spreadsheet/database:

  - Account ID

  - Form completion status (Complete/Incomplete)

  - Document match status (Match/No Match)

  - Verification status (Verified/Not Verified)

- Notes: Any anomalies or discrepancies found during the review process.

5. Reporting:

- Compile the findings and calculate the compliance rate.

- Prepare a report detailing the testing process, findings, and any recommendations for improvement.

- Discuss with the compliance team and update the risk management strategy as needed.

Creating a detailed compliance testing script is essential for an effective compliance testing program. By systematically defining the scope, identifying relevant controls, developing specific test steps, and defining clear success criteria, organizations can ensure they effectively manage and mitigate the risks associated with regulatory requirements. The example provided illustrates how a common document, like a Customer Account Opening Form, can be tested against multiple controls to ensure comprehensive compliance with AML regulations. This approach not only helps in maintaining regulatory compliance but also plays a crucial role in safeguarding the institution against potential financial crimes and reputational damage. This is only an example. These steps can be applied for any regulatory requirement, or internal policy requirement.

The example above illustrates why proper scoping of compliance tests is so important. As you can see from the example this is a detailed process that must be meticulously documented to evidence the review undertaken and also any potential issues noted.


## Re-Performance versus Outcome Testing

Within the scope of compliance testing, various methods can be employed to assess the effectiveness of controls and processes. Two significant methods are re-performance and outcome analysis. This discussion will explore these methods in detail, provide examples of each, and elucidate why they are important factors to consider when scoping compliance testing.

Understanding Re-performance and Outcome Analysis

"Re-performance" involves the tester independently executing the control or process as it was originally designed without relying on the work of others. This method allows the tester to verify firsthand whether the control effectively achieves its intended purpose under current conditions. It is akin to a "test drive" where the effectiveness of control is assessed by actively engaging with it rather than just reviewing outputs.

"Outcome analysis", on the other hand, focuses on examining the results or outputs of a process or control to determine if it meets the desired objectives. Unlike re-performance, where the process is actively executed, outcome analysis reviews existing data and documentation to evaluate the effectiveness based on outcomes. This method is more about analyzing the "footprints" left behind by a process, looking at what has been achieved.

Both methods serve crucial, albeit different, roles in compliance testing. Re-performance provides a hands-on confirmation that the processes and controls are functioning as expected when actively engaged. Outcome analysis offers insights based on the consequences of these processes, giving a broader view of their effectiveness over time.

Examples of Re-performance and Outcome Analysis

1. Re-performance Example in Financial Auditing:

   - Scenario: A compliance officer is testing an organization's expense reporting process. The control requires that all expense reports must be approved by a department manager before reimbursement.

- Re-performance: The compliance officer selects a sample of expense reports from the recent months. They re-perform the approval process by verifying that each report has a corresponding approval email or electronic signature from the designated manager as required by the policy.

- Importance: This direct engagement allows the auditor to confirm the integrity and operational effectiveness of the control at the point of testing, ensuring that the policy is not only in place but actively followed.

2. Outcome Analysis Example in Health and Safety Compliance:

- Scenario: A manufacturing company has implemented a new safety protocol to reduce workplace accidents. The protocol includes regular safety training sessions and upgraded safety equipment.

- Outcome Analysis: After a year, the compliance officer reviews the accident report logs, employee feedback, and health and safety inspection results to assess the effectiveness of the new safety protocol.

- Importance: By analyzing these outcomes, the company can determine if the introduction of the new safety measures has led to a tangible reduction in workplace accidents, thus assessing the real-world impact of their controls.

Importance in Compliance Testing Scope

When scoping compliance testing, it is critical to consider whether re-performance outcome analysis or a combination of both, is appropriate based on the nature of the control and the specific compliance requirements. Each method has its strengths and situations where it is most effective, influenced by factors such as the complexity of the control, the availability of data, and the potential consequences of failure.

1. Relevance to Control Type:

- Controls that are procedural and involve clear, step-by-step activities are often best tested through re-performance because it allows for a detailed examination of each step in the process.

- Controls that aim to achieve long-term strategic objectives might be better assessed through outcome analysis, as this method evaluates the effectiveness over a period and provides a bigger picture of the control's impact.

2. Data Availability and Integrity:

- Re-performance requires access to the processes and systems to actively engage with the control, which can be resource-intensive.

- Outcome analysis depends heavily on the availability and reliability of data. Inaccurate or incomplete data can skew the analysis, leading to misguided conclusions about the control's effectiveness.

3. Risk Considerations:

- High-risk areas may necessitate both methods to ensure a robust evaluation. For instance, in areas dealing with financial transactions or sensitive data, re-performing the control and analyzing its outcomes can provide a comprehensive view of both the operational integrity and the effectiveness in preventing breaches or losses.

4. Efficiency and Cost:

- The choice between re-performance and outcome analysis can also be influenced by cost considerations. Re-performance can be more costly and time-consuming than outcome analysis, which might leverage existing data and require less intensive resource investment.

In conclusion, scoping compliance testing involves a strategic decision on the methods to be used, with a clear understanding of what each method offers. Re-performance provides a granular, action-based verification of procedural compliance, while outcome analysis offers an overarching view of the control's effectiveness through its results. Choosing the right approach, or a combination of both, tailored to the specific requirements and risks of the organization, is essential for effective compliance testing, ensuring that controls are not only designed appropriately but are also delivering the desired outcomes.

## Sampling

One critical aspect of conducting effective compliance testing is the method of sampling used to select data or processes for testing. The choice of sampling method can significantly influence the results of the compliance testing, impacting both the reliability and validity of conclusions drawn. This section explores the different approaches to sampling in compliance testing, discusses the benefits and risks associated with each approach, delves into the importance of obtaining confidence levels, and underscores the necessity of documenting the sampling methodology.

Approaches to Sampling in Compliance Testing

1. Simple Random Sampling

- Description: Simple random sampling involves selecting items in such a way that every item has an equal chance of being chosen. This can be achieved using random number generators or drawing lots.

- Benefits: The primary benefit is its straightforwardness and the unbiased nature of the sample selection, making it easy to represent the larger population.

- Risks: The main risk is that without proper randomization processes, the sample may not be truly random, potentially leading to skewed results. Additionally, it might not cover all segments of the population effectively, especially if subgroups within the population vary significantly.

## 2. Stratified Sampling

- Description: In stratified sampling, the population is divided into subgroups (strata) that are homogenous but different from each other. A random sample is then drawn from each subgroup.

- Benefits: This approach improves the accuracy and representativeness of the sample by ensuring that specific, possibly critical, segments of the population are included in the sampling process.

- Risks: It requires accurate knowledge of the population characteristics to form appropriate strata. Misclassification or poor stratification can lead to biased results and reduce the effectiveness of the testing.

## 3. Cluster Sampling

- Description: Cluster sampling involves dividing the population into separate groups, known as clusters. A random sample of these clusters is selected, and data are collected from all members of the selected clusters.

- Benefits: Cluster sampling is cost-effective, especially when dealing with a large population spread over a wide geographic area.

- Risks: There is a higher potential for sampling error compared to other methods, particularly if the clusters themselves are not homogenous.

4. Systematic Sampling

- Description: Systematic sampling selects samples by following a fixed periodic interval (every nth item) from a randomly selected starting point within the population.

- Benefits: This method is simple to implement and ensures a spread across the entire population, making it more organized than simple random sampling.

- Risks: It can introduce periodicity biases, especially if there is a hidden pattern in the order of the population list that aligns with the sampling interval.

5. Judgmental Sampling (or Purposive Sampling)

- Description: Judgmental sampling relies on the judgment of the expert to select units that they believe are most useful or representative for the specific purpose of the study or test.

- Benefits: Useful in specialized testing where specific insights or expertise are needed to identify key risk areas.

- Risks: Highly susceptible to bias, as the sample selection is subjective, potentially leading to non-representative samples that do not accurately reflect the population.

<u>Importance of Obtaining Confidence Levels</u>

Confidence levels are a statistical measure that quantifies the probability that the sample results reflect the true population within a certain margin of error. In compliance testing, obtaining high confidence levels (typically 95% or 99%) is crucial as it strengthens the reliability of the testing conclusions. High confidence levels imply that there is a lesser chance that the sample results occurred by random fluctuations, and they provide assurance to the stakeholders that the conclusions drawn from the sample are likely to hold true for the entire population.

Components Influencing Confidence Levels:

1. Sample Size: The larger the sample size, the closer the sample mean gets to the population mean, which increases the reliability of the results.

2. Population Variability: Less variability (or standard deviation) within the population leads to a smaller margin of error, enhancing confidence in the results.

3. Z-score (Standard Score): This is a numerical measurement that describes a value's relationship to the mean of a group of values, measured in terms of standard deviations from the mean. The Z-score changes according to the desired confidence level (e.g., 1.96 for 95% confidence).

One tool that is free online that I have used to determine confidence levels can be located here: http://www.raosoft.com/samplesize.html. This tool is free and de-mystifies some of the math behind determining confidence levels (which is complex and a profession of its own). Using a tool like this and taking a pdf or screen shot of sample sizes calculated creates credibility in determining confidence levels.

Documenting the Methodology

Documenting the sampling methodology is critical for several reasons:

- Reproducibility: Proper documentation ensures that the testing process can be replicated, which is essential for verifying the results in audits or if the test needs to be rerun.

- Transparency: It provides transparency in how conclusions are drawn, which is important for building trust with regulatory bodies, auditors, and other stakeholders.

- Accountability: Detailed records hold the testing team accountable for their methodological choices and help in defending the testing process during regulatory reviews or legal challenges.

- Improvement: Documentation allows for retrospective analysis of what methods worked or did not work, informing improvements in future testing cycles.

The choice of sampling method in compliance testing has significant implications for the integrity and effectiveness of the testing process. Each method has its benefits and risks, and the choice should align with the specific objectives and conditions of the compliance test. Furthermore, achieving high confidence levels is essential for ensuring the reliability of the test results, and meticulous documentation of the sampling methodology is crucial for ensuring the process's transparency, reproducibility, and accountability.

## Exceptions

As we have discussed compliance testing scope, sampling and execution, we now turn to what happens when you find exceptions. An integral part of the compliance testing process is the identification and management of exceptions—instances where the company's practices do not meet the established standards. This section will delve into discussing the importance of documenting these exceptions, communicating findings to stakeholders, defending the findings, quantifying the issues, and finalizing results for formal reporting.

Documenting Exceptions

Thorough documentation of exceptions is crucial for several reasons:

- Record Keeping: It provides a historical record of findings that can be referenced in future audits or compliance reviews.

- Analysis and Remediation: Detailed records help in analyzing the root causes of exceptions and in devising effective remedial actions.

- Regulatory Requirements: In many industries, maintaining detailed compliance records is a regulatory requirement.

Effective documentation includes a description of the exception, the context in which it was found, the specific compliance standards violated, and any immediate actions taken. Compliance officers typically use standardized forms to ensure all relevant details are captured systematically. This can also be captured in the testing scripts discussed earlier.

Sharing Draft Findings with Stakeholders

Communicating the draft findings of compliance tests, especially exceptions, is a critical step in the compliance management process. Stakeholders—including management, the board of directors, and, in some instances, regulators —must be informed about the exceptions for several reasons:

- Transparency: It ensures that the decision-makers are aware of compliance risks and can make informed decisions.

- Resource Allocation: Helps in prioritizing areas that need more resources or immediate action.

- Accountability: Promotes a culture of compliance and accountability throughout the organization.

Communications should be clear concise, and include recommendations for addressing the exceptions (discussed more in the next Chapter, Issues/Exams). Meetings, detailed reports, and executive summaries are common methods used to share these findings.

Notice here the emphasis its on "draft" findings. Making sure preliminary findings are marked "draft" is important in that it gives stakeholders sufficient time to analyze and respond. Not providing this could create inaccuracies and foster distrust in the compliance testing program. There could be extenuating circumstances that the compliance tester was unaware of that could effect the exceptions noted.

<u>Defending Findings</u>

Being prepared to defend findings is essential, particularly in environments where the compliance results may be challenged by internal or external parties. Defending findings involves:

- Validation of Methods: Ensuring that the testing methods and processes are robust and can withstand scrutiny. This is why having a detailed description of the scope and methodology is crucial.

- Evidence-Based: Maintaining detailed evidence that supports each finding. This could include logs, documents, statements, and statistical analyses (e.g. testing scripts, sampling methodology).

- Expertise: Utilizing and, if necessary, presenting opinions from compliance experts or third-party validators to support the findings.

<u>Determining Statistics of Findings</u>

Quantifying exceptions is vital to understanding the scale and importance of compliance issues. For example, stating that "10 out of 100 accounts reviewed had exceptions" provides a clear measure of the extent of the problem and helps in assessing the risk exposure. Statistical analysis also helps in determining whether identified exceptions are isolated incidents or indicate a systemic problem.

Quantitative measures should be clear, verifiable, and based on sound statistical principles. The use of percentages, frequency distributions, and confidence intervals are common practices to help convey the significance of the findings to non-technical stakeholders.

Finalizing Results for Reporting

The final stage in the compliance testing process is compiling and finalizing the results for formal reporting. This will be discussed more in detail later in the chapter but should be noted here as the "exceptions" are generally the areas which obtain the most attention. This report should include:

- Executive Summary: A high-level overview of the testing process, key findings, and recommendations.

- Detailed Findings: An in-depth look at each exception found, its implications, and suggested corrective actions.

- Statistical Analysis: Presentation of the data in an understandable format, showing the extent of compliance issues.

- Recommendations for Future Action: Based on the findings, what steps should the organization take to improve compliance? (Discussed more in detail in the next chapter)

This report not only serves as a document for internal use but may also need to be submitted to regulatory bodies, depending on the industry and specific regulatory requirements.

Uncovering exceptions in compliance testing is a multifaceted process that requires meticulous planning, execution, and reporting. Each step, from documenting exceptions to communicating them to stakeholders and defending the findings, plays a critical role in strengthening the organization's compliance posture. Proper management of this process helps organizations not only to maintain compliance but also to enhance their operational integrity and preserve their reputation in the market.

## Drafting/Issuing Reports

Compliance testing reports are crucial documents that communicate the findings of compliance tests conducted within an organization. These reports provide insight into whether the organization adheres to legal, regulatory, and internal policy requirements. A well-drafted compliance testing report not only highlights areas of non-compliance but also facilitates the remediation process by providing clear and actionable information. This section delves into the specifics of drafting these reports, including understanding the audience, detailing what to include and what to exclude, managing disagreements over findings, and the role of compliance in the remediation process. Additionally, a practical example of a privacy compliance test with exceptions and proposed remediation is provided.

Audience for Compliance Testing Reports

The primary audience for compliance testing reports generally includes:

- Senior Management and Board of Directors: These stakeholders use the report to understand compliance risks facing the organization and to ensure that these risks are being managed appropriately.

- Compliance and Risk Management Teams: These teams need the details of the report to understand the specific areas of risk and non-compliance and to prioritize their remediation efforts.

- Internal Audit: This group uses the report to plan their audits and to cross-verify compliance health as part of their independent checks.

- Regulatory Bodies (if applicable): In certain regulated industries, reports might need to be submitted to oversight agencies to demonstrate compliance with legal requirements.

The report should be drafted keeping in mind the level of expertise and the information needs of each of these audiences. It should provide sufficient detail for compliance and risk management professionals while also summarizing key points for executive consumption.

<u>Content of the Compliance Testing Report</u>

A comprehensive compliance testing report should include the following:

- Executive Summary: This section provides a high-level overview of the testing scope, key findings, and critical recommendations. It should be succinct to cater to executive stakeholders who need to quickly grasp the essence of the report.

- Methodology: Clearly outline the sampling methods, tools, and processes used in the compliance testing to allow for reproducibility and transparency.

- Detailed Findings/Exceptions: Each finding or exception should be described in detail, including the nature of the non-compliance, the risks involved, and the impacted areas of the business.

- Recommendations for Remediation: For each exception noted, provide specific, actionable recommendations for how to address the deficiencies.

- Appendices and Supporting Documentation: Include detailed data, interview notes, and any other documents that support the findings and provide further detail.

Managing Disagreements Over Exceptions

Disagreements over exceptions noted in compliance tests can arise, particularly when the findings imply significant operational changes or financial costs. To manage such disagreements:

- Foster Open Communication: Encourage a culture where stakeholders feel open to express concerns and ask questions about the findings.

- Evidence-Based Discussions: Base all discussions on data and the documented evidence collected during the testing process.

- Mediation by an Independent Party: Sometimes, having an independent party (like an external auditor or a senior executive not directly involved in the processes tested) to review the findings can help resolve disputes.

- Follow-Up Meetings: Arrange meetings specifically aimed at discussing the contentious issues and exploring the implications of the findings more deeply.

Role of Compliance in Remediation

It's crucial to understand that while compliance teams are responsible for identifying and reporting on compliance risks and exceptions, they do not typically "own" the process of remediation. Remediation is generally the responsibility of the business unit or department where the exception was noted. The compliance team's role is to advise on regulatory requirements, monitor the remediation efforts, and re-test to ensure the effectiveness of the corrective actions undertaken. This will be discussed in greater length in the next chapter "Issues/Exams."

Below is an example of what a Compliance Testing Report might look like:

---

*Privacy Compliance Test*

Compliance Test Report: Privacy Policy Review

Executive Summary

This compliance test report presents the findings from a review of the privacy practices at [Company Name]. The audit aimed to assess compliance with the General Data Protection Regulation (GDPR) and the California Consumer Privacy Act (CCPA). The review uncovered two significant exceptions that could potentially impact the organization's compliance status and expose it to legal and reputational risks. Immediate action is recommended to address these deficiencies. This report provides a detailed analysis of each exception and outlines recommended strategies for remediation.

Methodology

The methodology for the privacy compliance test involved the following steps:

- Document Review: A thorough examination of all privacy policies, user consent forms, and third-party data-sharing agreements.

- System Audit: An inspection of the IT systems used to collect, store, and process personal data, ensuring they align with privacy standards.

- Interviews: Discussions with key personnel involved in data processing and policy formulation to understand the practical application of privacy policies.

- Sample Testing: Random checks were performed on user data to verify compliance with stated privacy practices and consent protocols.

The review was conducted over a three-week period (MM/DD/YY - MM/DD/YY), focusing on compliance with both GDPR and CCPA requirements.

Detailed Findings

Exception 1: Inadequate User Consent Mechanism

- Finding: The current user consent mechanism on the company's website does not allow users to give separate consents for different types of processing activities, which is a requirement under GDPR.

- Impact: This practice could lead to non-compliance with GDPR Article 7 regarding conditions for consent, potentially resulting in fines and damage to customer trust.

- Evidence: Screenshots of the consent banner, user account settings, and interviews with the web development team.

Exception 2: Insufficient Transparency in Data Sharing

- Finding: The privacy policy lacks specific details regarding the categories of third-party service providers with whom user data is shared, contrary to CCPA Section 1798.140.

- Impact: Non-disclosure of this information risks non-compliance with CCPA, leading to potential fines and legal challenges.

- Evidence: Review of the current Privacy Policy document and data sharing agreements with third parties.

Recommended Remediation Strategy

For Exception 1: Inadequate User Consent Mechanism

- Short-term Remediation: Update the consent mechanism on the website to include options for users to select their preferences for different types of data processing activities. This should be completed within the next 30 days.

- Long-term Strategy: Implement regular reviews and audits of the consent mechanism to ensure ongoing compliance with GDPR. Establish training programs for the web development team on compliance requirements.

For Exception 2: Insufficient Transparency in Data Sharing

- Short-term Remediation: Revise the Privacy Policy to include detailed information about the categories of third parties that may receive user data and the purposes for which they receive it. Aim to complete these revisions within 45 days.

- Long-term Strategy: Develop a protocol for regularly updating the Privacy Policy as new data-sharing agreements are established. Conduct annual training for the legal and compliance teams on CCPA requirements.

Appendix: Documents and Data Reviewed

1. Privacy Policy Document: The latest version of the privacy policy as it appears on the company website.

2. Consent Forms and User Interface Screenshots: Captures from various stages of the user interaction process where personal data is collected.

3. Data Sharing Agreements: Copies of contracts and agreements with third-party service providers.

4. Interview Transcripts: Summaries and key points from interviews with the IT team, legal advisors, and data protection officers.

Conclusion

This report highlights critical areas where [Company Name] must improve its privacy practices to ensure compliance with GDPR and CCPA. By addressing the identified exceptions promptly and adopting a proactive approach to privacy compliance, the company can safeguard itself against legal penalties and build stronger trust with its customers.

---

Drafting an effective compliance testing report is a critical skill for compliance professionals. It involves understanding the audience, carefully detailing the methodology and findings, and providing clear recommendations for remediation. By effectively communicating the outcomes of compliance tests, organizations can ensure that they not only meet regulatory requirements but also uphold high standards of operational integrity and ethical conduct. As you can see from the example above, these reports are comprehensive and professional in nature. Remember that the report is a reflection of the actions the compliance professional took to scope and execute the test. It should not only be a reflection of those actions but also a way for a compliance program to add value to an organization by helping it uncover issues and take remedial action without the involvement of a regulator. This is the most important way a compliance department can provide evidence to a regulator that it takes compliance seriously.

## Frequency of Tests

Like monitoring, compliance testing and compliance risk assessments are symbiotic. Understanding how these components interact can significantly enhance an organization's ability to manage and mitigate risks effectively. This section explores the connection between compliance testing and compliance risk assessments, focusing on how the frequency of testing is determined by residual risk and how outcomes from compliance testing can influence the evaluation of control effectiveness in risk assessments.

As discussed in the chapter on risk assessments, they typically categorize risks into high, medium, and low categories. This categorization is based on factors such as the inherent risk (consequences for non-compliance) and the control effectiveness (the adequacy of the controls to mitigate non-compliance), which gives us the residual risk.

Determining the Frequency of Compliance Testing Based on Residual Risk

One critical output of compliance risk assessments is the identification of residual risks. Residual risk is the level of risk that remains after controls are applied to mitigate the initial inherent risks identified. It essentially reflects the effectiveness of the control environment in managing identified risks to an acceptable level. Determining the frequency of compliance testing is directly influenced by these residual risk levels.

- High Residual Risk: Areas with high residual risk require more frequent compliance testing. This is because the consequences of non-compliance are potentially severe, and the existing controls may not be sufficiently reducing the risk. For example, in financial institutions, areas like anti-money laundering (AML) practices often carry high residual risks, given the dynamic nature of threat vectors and regulatory updates. Consequently, compliance tests in these areas might be scheduled quarterly or even monthly.

- Medium Residual Risk: For areas where the residual risk is assessed as medium, testing may be less frequent than in high-risk areas but still regular enough to ensure that controls are effective. These might be scheduled bi-annually or annually, depending on the specific circumstances and historical performance of the controls.

- Low Residual Risk: In areas where residual risks are low, the frequency of compliance testing might be reduced further. However, it remains important to conduct occasional tests to ensure that these risks do not escalate and that controls remain effective over time. Such testing might be biennial or triggered by significant changes in the operating environment or regulatory landscape.

Impact of Compliance Testing Outcomes on Control Effectiveness in Risk Assessments

Compliance testing directly influences the ongoing assessment of control effectiveness within the compliance risk assessment. By testing the operational effectiveness of compliance-related controls, organizations can obtain tangible evidence about whether these controls are working as intended or if there are gaps that need to be addressed.

- Identifying Control Weaknesses and Enhancements: The outcomes of compliance tests can reveal weaknesses in control designs or implementations. For instance, if a test of data privacy controls repeatedly finds unauthorized access to sensitive information, it indicates a need for stronger access controls or better training for employees on data handling practices. These findings feed back into the risk assessment process, potentially increasing the residual risk level and prompting a review of control frameworks.

- Adjusting Residual Risk Ratings: The results from compliance tests can lead to adjustments in residual risk ratings. For example, if compliance testing in an area previously considered high-risk shows consistent compliance over time, the residual risk rating for that area might be lowered. Conversely, if testing uncovers frequent or severe non-compliance issues, the residual risk rating might be increased.

- Evidence-Based Decision Making: Compliance testing provides evidence-based insights that help in making informed decisions about where to focus compliance efforts. This targeting of resources helps in optimizing the compliance function, ensuring that efforts and expenditures are directed toward areas where they are most needed, based on empirical evidence of risks and control effectiveness.

The symbiotic relationship between compliance testing and compliance risk assessments is central to an effective compliance program. The frequency of compliance testing is strategically determined based on the levels of residual risk identified during risk assessments. Moreover, the outcomes of these tests are crucial for evaluating and recalibrating the effectiveness of controls in managing identified risks. By closely integrating these two processes, organizations can ensure a robust compliance posture that not only detects and mitigates existing compliance risks but also dynamically adapts to new challenges and regulatory demands.

## Tools in Testing

The tools used in executing compliance testing programs can range from basic software like Microsoft Excel to more sophisticated compliance management systems. Each tool offers unique benefits and comes with its own set of risks. This essay explores these tools, discussing their advantages and disadvantages, and highlights the importance of documentation and the ability to track and manage the compliance testing process efficiently.

Simple Tools: Microsoft Excel

Benefits of Using Microsoft Excel:

1. Accessibility and Familiarity: Excel is widely used in business environments, making it an accessible option for many. Its familiar interface and flexible features allow users to start quickly without specialized training.

2. Flexibility: Excel's spreadsheet format is highly flexible, allowing users to create and customize data recording formats according to specific testing needs. Users can design templates for capturing data, calculating metrics, and reporting findings.

3. Cost-Effective: For many organizations, especially small and medium-sized enterprises, Excel is a cost-effective tool because it does not require additional investment if it is already part of the organization's software suite.

Risks Associated with Microsoft Excel:

1. Error-Prone: Manual data entry and spreadsheet formulas are susceptible to human error. Mistakes in data entry or formula configuration can lead to inaccurate results and misguided decisions.

2. Scalability Issues: Excel may not efficiently handle large datasets or complex analyses as it was not originally designed as a database system. Performance can degrade with larger files, and managing extensive data across multiple spreadsheets can become cumbersome.

3. Security Concerns: Spreadsheets lack robust built-in security features. Sensitive compliance data stored in Excel files might be at risk of unauthorized access or loss, especially if files are shared across multiple users without proper security measures.

Tailored Tools: Compliance Management Software

Benefits of Using Compliance Management Software:

1. Automation: Compliance management software typically includes automation features that streamline data collection, testing procedures, and reporting. Automation reduces the reliance on manual processes, thereby minimizing human errors and increasing efficiency.

2. Integrated Data Management: These tools are designed to handle large volumes of data, integrating data management and analysis within a single system. This integration facilitates better data integrity and consistency across various compliance testing activities.

3. Advanced Security Features: Compliance software often includes advanced security protocols, such as access controls, audit trails, and encryption, which help protect sensitive data against unauthorized access and data breaches.

Risks Associated with Compliance Management Software:

1. Complexity and Cost: Implementing specialized compliance software can be costly and complex, especially for smaller organizations. The initial setup, customization, and training can require significant investment in time and resources.

2. Over-reliance on Technology: There is a risk that employees may become overly reliant on the software, potentially neglecting the need for regular manual oversight and verification. This over-reliance can lead to complacency, where issues are overlooked because "the software is handling it."

3. Integration Challenges: Compliance software must often be integrated with other systems within the organization. This integration can be challenging, particularly if existing systems are outdated or based on incompatible technologies.

Importance of Documentation

Documentation plays a pivotal role in the success of compliance testing programs. Proper documentation ensures that every aspect of the compliance testing process is recorded, from the initial planning and scoping stages to the detailed results and follow-up actions. This documentation is crucial for several reasons:

- Audit Trail: Detailed records provide an audit trail that can be invaluable during internal or external audits. Auditors can review the documentation to verify that the compliance testing was conducted properly and that the findings are supported by evidence.

- Historical Records: Documentation serves as a historical record of compliance activities, which can be helpful for understanding trends over time and making informed decisions about future compliance strategies.

- Legal and Regulatory Compliance: In many industries, maintaining comprehensive records of compliance testing activities is a regulatory requirement. Failure to provide adequate documentation can result in penalties and damage to the organization's reputation.

Ability to Track and Manage the Process

Effective tracking and management of the compliance testing process are essential for ensuring that all tasks are completed on time and that issues are addressed promptly. Tools that offer dashboard capabilities, real-time monitoring, and alert systems can significantly enhance the management of compliance programs. These features help ensure that nothing falls through the cracks and that the organization remains in continuous compliance with all applicable laws and regulations.

Choosing the right tools for executing compliance testing programs depends on the specific needs, size, and resources of the organization. While simple tools like Microsoft Excel offer flexibility and are cost-effective, they come with limitations in scalability, security, and error reduction. More sophisticated compliance management software provides robust features for automation, security, and data integration but may require significant investment and adaptation. Regardless of the tools chosen, thorough documentation and effective management of the testing process are crucial for maintaining regulatory compliance and supporting the organization's long-term compliance goals.

## Conclusion of Chapter

As we conclude this chapter on compliance monitoring and testing, it is clear that these elements are not just fundamentals of an effective compliance program; they are their very backbone. In an era where regulatory environments are increasingly complex and dynamic, the need for robust compliance monitoring and testing is necessary. These activities provide the assurance that organizations not only meet all legal and regulatory requirements but also operate in a manner that upholds their ethical standards and protects their reputational integrity.

Compliance monitoring and testing are fundamental to identifying and mitigating risks that can lead to significant penalties, financial losses, and damage to reputation. Through continuous monitoring, organizations can maintain a constant vigil on their compliance status, swiftly identifying any deviations from required standards. This proactive approach is essential in today's fast-paced business environment, where regulatory changes occur frequently, and the scope for non-compliance issues can expand rapidly.

Similarly, compliance testing plays a critical role by providing a snapshot of the effectiveness of the organization's compliance controls. By systematically testing these controls against predefined criteria, organizations can evaluate whether their compliance frameworks are robust enough to manage and mitigate the identified risks. This process not only helps validate the efficacy of existing controls but also highlights areas where improvements are necessary.

Allocation of Resources

Given the critical importance of compliance monitoring and testing, it is imperative that these areas are where a compliance program allocates a significant amount of its time and resources. Investing in comprehensive monitoring and testing activities offers several key benefits:

- Risk Mitigation: Regular monitoring and rigorous testing of compliance controls significantly reduce the risk of non-compliance and its associated costs.

- Regulatory Adherence: Continuous compliance monitoring ensures that the organization remains in line with all relevant laws and regulations, which can change frequently and vary between jurisdictions.

- Operational Efficiency: By identifying inefficiencies and gaps in compliance processes, organizations can streamline operations, enhance internal controls, and improve overall operational efficiency.

- Stakeholder Confidence: Effective monitoring and testing build confidence among stakeholders, including investors, customers, and regulatory bodies, by demonstrating a commitment to compliance and ethical business practices.

Best Practices in Compliance Monitoring and Testing

To maximize the effectiveness of compliance monitoring and testing, organizations should consider the following best practices:

1. Tailored Approaches: Customize monitoring and testing activities to fit the unique risks and requirements of the organization. This involves understanding the specific regulatory landscape of the industry, as well as the organization's strategic objectives and operational nuances.

2. Technology: Utilize technology and/or compliance software tools that can automate and streamline monitoring and testing processes. These technologies can provide real-time data analysis and potentially generate automated alerts for potential compliance issues.

3. Skilled Personnel: Ensure that the team responsible for compliance monitoring and testing is adequately trained and possesses the necessary expertise. Continuous training and professional development are crucial in keeping the compliance team updated with the latest regulatory changes and best practices.

4. Continuous Improvement: Use the insights gained from monitoring and testing activities to continuously improve the compliance program. This involves regularly updating the risk assessment methodologies, refining testing processes, and enhancing the overall compliance strategy based on practical insights and industry trends.

5. Transparent Reporting: Maintain transparency in reporting the findings from monitoring and testing activities to internal and external stakeholders. This transparency helps in building trust and ensures that all stakeholders are informed about the organization's compliance health.

In conclusion, compliance monitoring and testing are not merely regulatory requirements—they are strategic imperatives. An organization's ability to effectively monitor and test its compliance controls directly impacts its capability to navigate the complex regulatory waters of the global business environment. By dedicating sufficient resources to these critical areas, organizations can ensure that they not only prevent costly compliance failures but also foster a culture of integrity and compliance that enhances their market reputation and operational success.

Thus, as we reflect on the importance of compliance monitoring and testing, it becomes evident that these activities should be viewed as investments in the organization's future. They are essential for safeguarding against compliance risks, enabling sustainable business practices, and ultimately driving long-term success.

# Issues and Exams

## Issues

As we learned in the last chapter on Monitoring and Testing, these activities may result in uncovering exceptions referred to as "issues" with processes, controls, or outcomes. Just what is an "Issue"? In some jurisdictions, this may also be coined a "Breach" or a "Finding." In this section, we discuss the role of compliance, tracking, potential regulatory impact and the potential to "re-test" after remediation efforts have concluded. This is part of the fundamentals of compliance because it is not a compliance department's job simply to identify issues and then walk away. Compliance needs to advise the business on how issues can be resolved regardless of wether they own the process.

## Role of Compliance in Remediation

As discussed prior, compliance monitoring and testing programs are essential tools for identifying and assessing areas where an organization may be at risk of non-compliance. Once issues are uncovered, the remediation process begins—a phase where the roles and responsibilities of different organizational units are distinctly delineated. This section explores the specific role of compliance in advising on the remediation of issues uncovered during these programs, highlighting how the actual remediation is managed by process owners while compliance maintains an advisory position.

Once a compliance issue is identified, the process transitions from detection to remediation. It is at this juncture that the distinction between the roles of compliance and process owners becomes particularly significant. Compliance's role is advisory; they do not "own" the remediation process but guide and recommend corrective actions to those who do.

The remediation responsibility lies firmly with the process owners—the managers or department heads who oversee the day-to-day execution of the implicated processes or control. This division of responsibilities ensures that remediation measures are applied directly by those with the most comprehensive understanding of the processes and the operational capacity to implement changes effectively.

Compliance's advisory role involves interpreting regulatory requirements and providing a roadmap for compliance that aligns with both the spirit and the letter of the law. This includes suggesting corrective actions, helping to prioritize remediation efforts based on risk exposure, and providing expertise on regulatory nuances. Compliance officers also ensure that process owners are equipped with the knowledge and tools necessary to correct the course. This might involve training sessions, written guidelines, and regular consultations.

For remediation to be effective, it must be owned by the process owner but governed by clear guidelines and recommendations from the compliance department. This cooperative relationship ensures that remediation efforts are both appropriate and timely.

Role of Process Owners:

Process owners must take active ownership of the remediation tasks. This involves:

- Understanding the implications of the compliance findings.

- Developing and implementing corrective actions.

- Allocating resources and setting timelines for remediation efforts.

- Communicating progress and challenges back to the compliance department.

Compliance's Supporting Role:

While process owners manage the remediation, compliance's advisory role is continuous. They must:

- Provide ongoing guidance on regulatory requirements.

- Offer expertise in developing corrective measures.

- Monitor the implementation of remediation efforts to ensure compliance.

- Update training and documentation to reflect new practices.

This dual approach not only ensures compliance but also fosters a culture of continuous improvement and accountability within the organization.

The role of compliance in the remediation of issues uncovered during monitoring and testing programs is fundamentally advisory. While compliance professionals identify issues and guide the remediation process, the ownership of the actual remediation lies with the process owners. This clear division of roles ensures that remediation efforts are directly managed by those with the operational knowledge and responsibility for the processes, while compliance provides the necessary regulatory framework and support. This structure is essential for effective compliance management and helps organizations maintain high standards of integrity and adherence to regulatory requirements.

# Issue Tracking

Once monitoring and testing activities identify issues or breaches, the subsequent phase—issue remediation—begins. As discussed above, while compliance teams do not own the remediation process, their role in tracking and overseeing its progress is crucial. This tracking ensures that remediation efforts are effective, timely, and aligned with both regulatory expectations and organizational objectives.

Essential Functions of Compliance in Remediation Tracking

1. Ensuring Accountability:

Compliance teams hold the organization accountable for implementting remediation measures identified during monitoring and testing. By keeping a diligent record and tracking the progress of these remediations, compliance ensures that no identified issue is overlooked or inadequately addressed. This role is critical because it impacts the organization's ability to operate within the bounds of legal and ethical standards. Compliance officers facilitate regular updates and reviews, ensuring that process owners are on track and deviations are reported and escalated as necessary.

2. Providing a Clear Audit Trail:

A systematic tracking process creates a comprehensive audit trail that details how each identified issue is being addressed. This audit trail is crucial not only for internal review but also for demonstrating due diligence to external regulators and auditors. It helps in establishing a history of compliance and can be invaluable during regulatory inspections or audits, where evidence of proactive remediation needs to be shown. Compliance's involvement guarantees that the documentation is thorough, accurate, and reflective of all actions taken.

3. Assessing the Effectiveness of Remediations:

Compliance does not just track whether remediation is completed; it also evaluates the effectiveness of these efforts. This could involve re-testing or follow-up reviews (discussed more below) to ensure that the corrective actions have indeed resolved the issues without introducing new problems. Through this continuous assessment, compliance departments help the organization maintain a dynamic approach to risk management, adjusting strategies as new information or technologies become available.

4. Risk Management and Mitigation:

The role of compliance in tracking issue remediation is integral to broader risk management strategies. By monitoring how remediations are handled, compliance can identify patterns or systemic issues that may indicate deeper risks within the organization. This insight allows for the development of more robust risk mitigation strategies and preventive measures, reducing the likelihood of future non-compliance.

5. Facilitating Continuous Improvement:

Tracking the progress and effectiveness of remediation efforts fosters a culture of continuous improvement within the organization. Compliance departments use the data and outcomes from tracking to inform training programs, update policies, and refine risk assessments. This not only helps in adapting to changing regulatory environments but also enhances the overall resilience and compliance posture of the organization.

The role of compliance in tracking issue remediation is fundamental to effective compliance management. This responsibility ensures that remediation processes are not only implemented but are also effective and aligned with the organization's compliance goals. Compliance teams, through meticulous tracking, provide a critical check on the organization's operations, safeguarding against potential financial, legal, and reputational risks. By ensuring that issues identified in monitoring and testing are resolved appropriately, compliance supports the organization in maintaining its integrity and upholding its commitment to adhere to all applicable laws and regulations.

## Determination of Regulatory Impact

Before the initiation of monitoring and testing activities or during the process of uncovering issues, the fundamental responsibility of the compliance department is to evaluate the regulatory impact of the issues identified. This evaluation is crucial as it informs the subsequent steps of the compliance process, including the urgency and manner of remediation required. When assessing the regulatory impact, compliance must consider a multifaceted set of factors that influence both the approach to and the prioritization of the remediation efforts.

Key Considerations in Determining Regulatory Impact

1. Regulatory Priorities:

One of the primary considerations is whether the issue aligns with current regulatory priorities. Regulatory bodies often highlight specific areas of concern or focus depending on emerging risks, economic changes, or policy shifts. If the issue falls within these highlighted areas, it may warrant more immediate and stringent remediation efforts due to heightened regulatory scrutiny. Fro example, issues uncovered pertaining to Privacy violations may warrant more scrutiny than a small delay in a regulatory filing uncovered.

2. Risk Ratings in Compliance Risk Assessment:

Another critical factor is the residual risk rating of the rule or regulation implicated by the issue, as identified in the organization's compliance risk assessment. This assessment helps in quantifying the potential impact of non-compliance. Issues linked to regulations that carry a high residual risk score typically require more urgent attention to mitigate potential damage or penalties.

3. Client Impact:

The level and nature of clients impacted by the issue also play a critical role in determining its regulatory impact. Issues that affect vulnerable clients or a significant portion of the client base may demand a more robust response to protect client interests and maintain trust in the organization. This aspect also influences whether there is a need for client notification, which can have legal and reputational implications.

4. Notification Requirements:

Determining whether the issue necessitates notifying regulatory bodies or clients is paramount. Some regulations require prompt disclosure of certain types of breaches or failures (e.g. cybersecurity breaches). Compliance must assess whether the issue meets the threshold for such disclosures, which can prevent additional penalties and mitigate reputational damage.

5. Repeat Issues and Findings:

The historical context of the issue, particularly whether it is a repeat finding, significantly affects the compliance risk assessment. Repeat issues indicate systemic problems and can trigger more severe regulatory actions, including higher fines and more stringent oversight. They also necessitate higher levels of internal escalation and potentially broader organizational changes to address the root causes.

6. Level of Escalation Required:

The level of escalation needed within the organization is also a vital consideration. This depends on the severity and scope of the issue, the areas of the business affected, and the potential for harm. High-impact issues may require involvement from senior management or the board, especially if they affect critical business operations or pose significant reputational risks.

Additional Factors Based on Organizational Complexity and Industry

The complexity of the organization and the specific industry in which it operates may introduce additional factors to be considered. For example, in highly regulated industries like banking or pharmaceuticals, compliance might need to evaluate additional layers of regulatory requirements or international guidelines. Similarly, the organizational structure (such as decentralized operations) can complicate the assessment and remediation of compliance issues.

The determination of the regulatory impact of uncovered issues by the compliance department is a comprehensive process that requires evaluating multiple factors. This assessment directs the prioritization and strategy of remediation efforts, ensuring that the organization addresses compliance issues effectively and aligns with both regulatory expectations and business integrity.

## Re-testing Upon Completion of Remediation

Once remediation efforts have been addressed, it is prudent for the compliance department to consider the necessity and scope of performing a test on the newly implemented or modified process. This testing phase is critical to ensure that the remediation has effectively addressed the compliance issues without introducing new problems. However, such re-testing should not be automatically conducted for every remediation but should be carefully considered based on specific criteria to optimize resources and focus efforts where they are most needed.

Factors Influencing the Decision to Perform Re-testing

1. Regulatory Impact:

The first factor to consider is the regulatory impact of the original issue (as discussed above). If the issue had a high regulatory impact, implying significant potential penalties or severe reputational risk, re-testing becomes crucial. This ensures that the organization is now fully compliant and that similar risks are mitigated moving forward. High-impact issues often warrant more stringent follow-up to demonstrate to regulators and stakeholders that the organization takes compliance seriously.

2. Nature of the Internal Control Impacted:

The second factor involves the nature of the internal control that was impacted by the original compliance issue. Controls can be manual or automated, each with different risk profiles and testing requirements. Automated controls may require testing to ensure the software or system updates are functioning as expected, while manual controls often need checks to verify that procedural changes are being followed by staff. Additionally, the type of control—whether it is preventative or detective—also dictates the testing approach. Preventative controls are designed to stop errors or violations before they occur, making their correct functioning crucial, whereas detective controls are meant to identify and address issues after they have occurred.

3. Number of Clients Impacted:

The scale of the impact on clients also determines the need for re-testing. If a wide range of clients were affected by the original issue, ensuring that the remediation has comprehensively addressed all potential client impacts is essential. This helps in maintaining client trust and satisfaction, critical elements in client retention and business success.

4. Remuneration Provided as a result of the Issue:

If the issue leads to remuneration or compensation being paid to affected parties, re-testing becomes more significant. This is because the need for renumeration often indicates a serious lapse in compliance or control effectiveness. Re-testing in such scenarios ensures that the remedial actions have adequately addressed the root causes of the issue to prevent future occurrences.

Structured Format for Re-testing

Re-testing should be conducted in a structured format to ensure thoroughness and reliability (as discussed in the prior chapter). This involves defining clear testing criteria, employing systematic testing procedures, and documenting results comprehensively. A structured approach not only provides a clear pathway for testing but also helps in maintaining consistency and objectivity in the evaluation of new or altered processes.

Escalation of Uncovered Issues

Any issues uncovered during the re-testing phase should be escalated immediately. Quick escalation is crucial for addressing potential failures in the remediation efforts and for making necessary adjustments promptly. Alongside escalation, a thorough determination of the root causes of any failures found during re-testing should be conducted. Understanding these root causes is essential for implementing more effective long-term solutions and for continuous improvement in compliance processes.

The decision to re-test a remediated process in compliance should be based on a combination of factors, including the regulatory impact, the nature of the impacted control, the breadth of client impact, and the presence of renumeration related to the original issue. By considering these factors, compliance departments can strategically allocate resources to testing efforts that ensure the organization not only meets regulatory requirements but also upholds high standards of operational integrity and customer trust.

## Examinations

Whether its a phone call, email, or registered mail, the time will come when your firm will be examined by a regulator. Perhaps you work in an industry where this does not happen on a frequent basis, or if you are in the Banking industry, you may be used to having regulators on site. It is inevitable. This section will touch on the different types of examinations and the role that compliance plays during an examination. It will discuss how to manage document requests, on-site visits, interviews, and findings, including potential enforcement actions. These are all valuable skills that your organization will look to compliance to manage. To be clear, compliance manages the exam but should not be blamed if findings should occur unless the compliance department failed to fulfill its duties within the firm. During the examination process, compliance is akin to a shepherd, and the different department leaders are its flock. Compliance should be preparing individuals for expectations during the exam and make sure that information is provided in a timely and accurate manner. This is a good time for the compliance department to show its value and will also take a significant amount of resources. I cant tell you the number of times I had to work late, or on weekends, to help facilitate a smooth examination with a regulator. The key is to be prepared and organized. The organization will make record production more efficient.

## Types of Exams

There are three primary types of regulatory examinations: routine exams, sweep exams, and targeted exams. Each type serves a unique purpose and requires a specific approach from the organizations being examined. Understanding the distinctions among these exams is essential for effective preparation and management.

Routine Exams

Routine examinations are conducted on a predetermined cycle, such as annually, biannually or on a determined cycle (e.g. every 4 years), depending on the regulatory body's guidelines or the organization's past compliance history. These exams are comprehensive, covering a wide range of areas within an organization to ensure overall compliance with applicable regulations. They are generally risk-based in nature but will be much more comprehensive than a sweep or targeted examination.

Organizations should maintain a constant state of readiness for routine exams by implementing ongoing compliance checks and balances. Regular internal audits and reviews should mimic the rigors of a routine regulatory examination to identify and rectify compliance issues proactively. Effective document management systems should be in place to ensure that all necessary documentation is readily accessible and up-to-date, thereby facilitating smooth document production during the exam.

Sweep Exams

Sweep exams are not based on a regular schedule but are triggered by emerging market trends or issues identified across an industry sector. Regulatory bodies conduct these exams when they perceive a potential widespread risk to the market or consumers, often focusing on specific compliance areas like trading practices or disclosure requirements.

The key to managing sweep exams is staying informed about industry trends and potential regulatory focuses. Organizations should monitor guidance from regulatory bodies and adjust their compliance programs accordingly. It is also crucial to train staff in areas prone to regulatory scrutiny based on current trends. Since sweep exams can arise unexpectedly, having a rapid response plan for document production and staff briefing can significantly ease the process.

Targeted Exams

Targeted examinations are initiated in response to specific triggers such as suspicious activities, complaints, significant operational changes, or negative media coverage. These exams are more focused than routine or sweep exams, often zeroing in on a particular aspect of the business where issues are suspected.

To effectively manage targeted exams, organizations must be agile and focused in their response. It is essential to understand the scope of the exam quickly and mobilize the right resources to address the regulator's concerns. This might involve isolating documents, data, and personnel related to the area under examination. Organizations should also conduct a pre-exam risk assessment in the targeted area to anticipate potential findings and prepare explanations or corrective actions in advance.

Differences and Document Production

While all three types of exams require robust document production, the scope and specificity of the documentation can vary significantly. Routine exams might require a broad array of records reflecting the overall health of the compliance program, while targeted exams require in-depth information about a specific issue or business unit. Sweep exams, on the other hand, demand documentation related to particular practices or transactions that are currently under regulatory scrutiny industry-wide.

Each type of regulatory examination presents unique challenges and requires tailored management strategies. By understanding the nuances of routine, sweep, and targeted exams, organizations can better prepare for and respond to regulatory scrutiny, ensuring compliance and mitigating risks associated with non-compliance. Effective preparation includes maintaining comprehensive, up-to-date documentation and training staff to handle inquiries and provide necessary information swiftly and accurately during an exam.

## Document Production

Document production in response to records requests from regulators is a complex and resource-intensive process, requiring meticulous planning and execution. The challenges can vary greatly depending on the volume and specificity of the data requested, as well as the format in which it needs to be delivered—be it electronic or physical.

Challenges in Document Production

1. Scope of Request:

Regulators may request extensive ranges of data or information that necessitate considerable effort to compile. Such requests can span multiple departments or touch on sensitive areas of operation, requiring collaboration across various segments of the organization to ensure complete and accurate production.

2. Format of Production:

The format required for document submission can significantly affect the complexity of the task. Electronic records are generally easier to handle, search, and transmit but may require data extraction, conversion, and encryption efforts. Physical documents, on the other hand, require careful handling to ensure that they are preserved in their original state, correctly cataloged, and securely transported.

3. Privileged Information:

A critical aspect of document production is the identification and handling of attorney-client privileged communications. Care must be taken to review all documents for privileged content, as inadvertent production could waive the privilege and expose sensitive legal communications to scrutiny.

Managing Large-scale Requests: Rolling Production

For particularly voluminous requests, regulators may agree to, or an organization may propose a "rolling production" schedule. This method involves providing requested documents in segments over a specified timeline, allowing for continuous processing and review. This approach can help manage workload and ensure each batch of documents is thoroughly vetted for accuracy and completeness before submission.

Handling Inaccessible Documents

In instances where an organization is unable to locate requested documents—due to their destruction, loss, or improper maintenance—the situation must be handled with transparency and urgency. The best course of action is to notify the regulator promptly about the issue. Depending on the circumstances, it may be possible to recreate the documents from other sources, though this needs to be clearly communicated and agreed upon with the regulatory body. Be prepared to cite the root cause of any documents that cannot be located and formulate remedial action swiftly to assure regulators the problem will not persist. This may also be a good time to alert outside counsel as it could result in an enforcement action.

Resource Allocation and Internal Communication

The effort to gather and produce documents involves not just the compliance team but also IT, legal, records management personnel, operations, finance, sales, and others. Allocating sufficient resources and setting realistic timelines are crucial. Communicating these timelines to involved parties internally is vital to set clear expectations and ensure that all team members are aligned with the production schedule.

Extensions and Regulatory Interaction

While it is possible to request extensions from regulators, this should be done sparingly. Frequent requests for extensions can give the impression of disorganization or, worse, non-compliance. Therefore, it's crucial to use extensions as a last resort and ensure that when requested, they are well justified and backed by a clear plan for meeting the new deadlines.

Review Prior to Production

If possible, someone from compliance or potentially legal should review all documents prior to producing them to a regulator. This will help in uncovering any potential issues the regulator may find with the document produced. It is important to scrutinize these documents as a regulator would think about what they might look for. Of course, in overly large data sets or physical productions, this may not be possible if meeting tight deadlines. In those instances, a risk-based approach should be used. Look for samples based on areas of risk or take random samples and look for issues. Do not under any circumstances try to change or alter the document prior to submission to regulators. There are too many enforcement actions to mention where that has been attempted, and it does not end well, for the individual and the organization. Rather identify the issue, determine its root cause, and come up with a potential response and remediation plan.

Effective document production for regulatory requests is an essential but challenging aspect of compliance. It requires detailed planning, cross-departmental cooperation, and clear communication both internally and with the regulator. By understanding these complexities and preparing accordingly, organizations can manage this process efficiently, maintaining compliance and upholding their reputations in the regulatory community.

## On-Site Visitations

During regulatory examinations, the logistics and dynamics of hosting examiners can significantly influence the efficiency and effectiveness of the process. Whether examiners visit physically or conduct their assessments virtually, organizations must strategically plan how to accommodate and manage their presence. The move towards on-site examinations, reemphasized post-Covid, underscores the importance of direct interactions in assessing the compliance environment and operational workflows. This section will explore various considerations, such as the logistics of hosting examiners on-site, communicating their presence to staff, and optimal interaction protocols for compliance personnel.

<u>Hosting Examiners On-Site</u>

1. Preparation of Physical Space:

Selecting an appropriate space to host examiners is crucial. The chosen area should ensure privacy and access to necessary technological resources, such as secure internet access, printers, and telephones. This space should ideally be separate from main operational areas to minimize disruption to daily activities and safeguard sensitive information. If the exam is expected to last several days or weeks, consider conveniences like access to restrooms and proximity to break rooms. You may be inclined to put examiners in the basement or in other potentially uncomfortable settings (e.g. rooms that are frequently too warm or too cold). I would highly discourage you from taking this approach. While I realize not every organization has an abundant amount of space, placing them in a comfortable setting is ideal. Intentionally making them uncomfortable will only sow distrust and frustration, which could affect their review.

2. Security and Access Controls:

Implementing proper security measures is essential to control access to the designated examination area. This may involve issuing temporary badges or access codes and ensuring that only authorized personnel can enter the examination space. These measures help maintain the integrity of the examination process and protect sensitive company data.

<u>Communicating the Examination to Staff</u>

1. Initial Notification:

It's vital to inform staff about the upcoming examination and the presence of regulators on-site. This communication should be clear about the timing, expected duration, and areas of focus for the examination. It should also outline expected behavior and protocols for interacting with the examiners. Let the staff know where the examiners will be sitting, how they should interact with them, and what to do if they are approached by them (e.g. reroute them to compliance).

2. Ongoing Updates:

Keeping staff updated throughout the examination process helps manage expectations and reduce anxiety or disruptions. Updates can be communicated via email or brief meetings, depending on the length of the exam and the level of staff involvement.

<u>Compliance Interaction with On-Site Examiners</u>

1. Daily Check-Ins:

Scheduling daily check-ins with regulatory examiners can be highly beneficial. These meetings provide an opportunity to address any questions or concerns that have arisen during the day and to clarify any information the examiners may need. It also allows the compliance team to gauge the progress of the examination and anticipate potential areas of concern that may require additional attention.

2. Documentation and Assistance:

The compliance team should be prepared to provide documentation and explanations promptly. This responsiveness not only facilitates the examination process but also demonstrates the organization's commitment to compliance and transparency.

3. Managing Interactions:

Guiding how employees interact with examiners is crucial. Employees should be instructed to be cooperative and courteous but also reminded to direct technical or sensitive questions to the compliance team. This helps ensure that information is communicated centrally, accurately and consistently.

4. Post-Examination Debrief:

After the examination concludes, organizing a debrief with the compliance team and key personnel involved in the exam can provide valuable insights. This session should review the examiners' feedback, discuss any preliminary findings, and start planning for any necessary remediation actions.

The presence of regulators on-site for examinations is a significant event that requires careful planning and management. By adequately preparing the physical space, effectively communicating with staff, and managing daily interactions through structured check-ins, organizations can ensure that the examination process is as smooth and productive as possible. This proactive approach not only supports the immediate needs of the regulatory examination but also strengthens the organization's overall compliance culture.

## Interviews

Preparing for and managing interviews during regulatory examinations is a critical aspect that organizations must handle with care and strategic foresight. These interviews are not merely formalities but pivotal moments during which examiners gather insights into the organization's operations, compliance practices, and potential areas of concern. The role of compliance in this context is not only advisory but also protective, ensuring that interviewees are adequately prepared and that the organization's interests are safeguarded throughout the process.

Preparing Key Staff for Interviews

The initial step in preparing for interviews involves ensuring that all potential interviewees are thoroughly knowledgeable about their respective areas. This includes understanding the processes, products, or regulatory requirements pertinent to their roles. Compliance should assess the level of preparedness of each individual and provide additional training or information sessions if gaps are identified.

Conducting mock interviews can be an invaluable preparation tool. In these sessions, someone from the compliance team can simulate the role of an examiner, posing likely questions and scenarios. This exercise helps interviewees become accustomed to the format of the questions and the environment of the interview, reducing anxiety and improving response quality. It also allows compliance to gauge how well individuals can articulate their knowledge and identify any areas where further clarification of facts or processes is necessary.

Interviewees should be briefed on effective communication techniques during interviews. This includes understanding how to limit their answers to exactly what is asked without volunteering additional information, which might inadvertently lead to further scrutiny or complications. They should also be comfortable with utilizing pauses or silence in their responses, and they must know that it is acceptable to say "I don't know" when unsure about an answer rather than speculating or providing incorrect information.

During the Interview

It is advisable for a member of the compliance team to be present during actual interviews. This presence ensures that the legal rights of the employee and the organization are maintained and that interviews do not stray into inappropriate or irrelevant areas. Compliance can guide the interviewee, intervene if questions become misleading or inappropriate, and help keep the discussion focused on the relevant topics.

After the Interview

Following each interview, a quick debriefing session should be conducted. This session is an opportunity to review how the interview went, discuss any concerns the interviewee might have, and examine the notes taken by the compliance member who was present. This review can help identify any areas that might require follow-up information or clarification to the regulators.

Engaging Outside Expertise

In situations where the stakes are particularly high or where the organizational capabilities are limited in dealing with complex regulatory issues, it might be beneficial to hire outside counsel or a consultant. These professionals can offer specialized expertise in preparing staff for regulatory interviews, developing effective communication strategies, and ensuring that the organization's responses are legally prudent and tactically sound.

Interviews during regulatory examinations are crucial moments that can significantly influence the outcome of the examination. Compliance departments play an essential role in ensuring that all interviewees are properly prepared, that the interviews are conducted in a controlled and lawful manner, and that any information gaps identified during the interviews are addressed promptly. Through meticulous preparation and strategic management of the interview process, organizations can navigate regulatory examinations more effectively, reducing the risk of adverse findings and reinforcing their commitment to compliance.

# Findings

When examiners conclude their review and prepare to issue their findings, the manner in which these findings are reported—whether as a draft or a final report—significantly impacts the subsequent actions of a compliance team. This phase is critical as it represents a potential turning point in the regulatory examination process. Understanding how to navigate both the draft and final stages of the reporting process can significantly influence the outcome and future regulatory relationships.

<u>Draft Findings Report</u>

Opportunity for Dispute:

If regulators provide a draft findings report, this serves as a crucial opportunity for the organization to address and potentially dispute any findings before they are finalized. This can be pivotal in mitigating the severity of any sanctions or required remedial actions. Disputes can be based on several grounds:

- Additional Documentation: Sometimes, relevant documents or evidence may not have been reviewed by the regulator during the initial examination. Providing these can clarify misunderstandings or support the organization's case.

- Clarification of Misunderstandings: If information has been misinterpreted, additional detailed explanations can help correct any inaccuracies in the report.

- Scope of Regulator's Purview: Arguing that certain findings fall outside the regulatory scope can be another ground for dispute, although this requires a robust understanding of regulatory boundaries and mandates. If you feel this is occurring, it is best to get Outside Counsel involved to assist.

Strategic Dispute Management:

Choosing to dispute findings should be a well-considered decision. While it is important to correct inaccuracies, it is equally crucial to maintain a cooperative and respectful relationship with the regulator. Disputes should be factual, well-documented, and presented professionally. In cases of fundamental disagreement, escalating the issue to a higher authority within the regulatory agency could be considered. However, this should be approached cautiously, as it could affect the organization's relationship with the regulator.

<u>Final Report and Response</u>

1. Response Preparation:

Once findings are finalized, drafting a comprehensive response is essential. This response should address each finding individually, outlining the steps the organization plans to take, including:

- Specific Remedial Actions: Clearly describe what actions will be taken to address each finding.

- Responsibility Assignment: Specify who within the organization will own each remedial action. This ensures accountability.

- Timelines: Set realistic timelines for the completion of these actions. It is better to allow extra time and complete the action early than to risk a delay.

2. Socialization of Responses:

Before finalizing the response, it is crucial to review and agree upon the content with all impacted stakeholders and senior management. This ensures that all parts of the organization are aligned and committed to the remediation plans.

1. Compliance Oversight:

Compliance should actively track the progress of remediation efforts against the timelines and commitments made in the response. Regular updates should be communicated to both internal stakeholders and, when necessary, to the regulator.

2. Managing Delays:

If remediation timelines are at risk, it is important to promptly notify the regulator, explaining the root cause of the delay and providing a revised timeline. Frequent delays can damage the organization's credibility and should be avoided.

3. Record Keeping:

Maintaining detailed records of all remediation efforts is crucial. These records will likely be the first point of reference in any future examinations and can help prevent repeat findings.

Navigating the post-examination phase effectively involves a careful balance of dispute management, precise communication, and diligent follow-through on remediation efforts. Ensuring accuracy in response to regulatory findings and maintaining robust documentation is key to demonstrating a strong culture of compliance and can influence the scope and nature of future regulatory interactions. This proactive and transparent approach not only addresses current regulatory concerns but also strengthens the organization's overall compliance posture.

## Enfoncement Actions

Receiving a notification from the enforcement department of a regulator is a serious matter and warrants immediate escalation to the legal department of the organization or outside counsel if no legal department exists. Enforcement proceedings are complex and specialized, often involving intricate legal interpretations and procedural nuances best handled by experienced legal professionals. The legal department or outside counsel should take the lead in managing these proceedings to ensure that the organization's responses are legally sound and effectively communicated. Compliance departments play a supportive yet crucial role by providing essential documentation, detailed narratives of the findings, comprehensive descriptions of internal controls, and copies of risk assessments, along with records of monitoring and testing efforts. This collaborative approach ensures that all factual and procedural elements are accurately represented and legally vetted.

It is imperative for the compliance team to maintain close coordination with the legal department throughout the duration of the enforcement proceedings. While legal professionals handle the intricacies of legal arguments and procedural compliance, the role of the compliance team is to ensure that all relevant information and documentation are readily available and that any ongoing remediation efforts are communicated to legal. This helps legal counsel present a well-rounded defense or response armed with the latest compliance efforts and internal changes. Given the potential duration of these proceedings, which can extend over months or even years, maintaining a streamlined communication channel between compliance and legal is essential for adapting strategies in response to developments within the enforcement process.

The organizational strategy for handling updates and communications about ongoing enforcement actions must be carefully managed to maintain confidentiality and legal privilege. It's important to decide early on who within the organization will be responsible for communicating updates to various stakeholders, including executive management and potentially affected departments. This planning helps in managing expectations and ensures consistent messaging that adheres to legal advice. Keeping these communications under the strict guidance of legal counsel helps safeguard the organization against potential breaches of privilege or inadvertent disclosures. Understanding that enforcement actions are a common part of regulatory oversight, as evidenced by entities like the SEC collecting over $4.9 billion in enforcement actions in 2023, should reassure organizations that with the right legal and compliance strategies, they can navigate these proceedings effectively.

## Conclusion

In conclusion, compliance plays a vital role in issue remediation and regulatory examinations. From playing the role of adviser during issue remediation efforts to acting as the liaison during examinations, compliance should be strategic and prepared. While these two items are different in nature, they are combined due to their nature in the Fundamentals of Compliance and play an important role in any compliance program. Particularly the management of regulatory examinations. This will be a considerable effort which is not built into the day to day activities of a functional compliance program. Be prepared to expend significant resources when exams get announced, even if they are expected. If you are in a highly regulated industry where examinations occur frequently, you may want to consider making the management of those exams someones full-time job. Examinations are only one part of the Fundamentals of Compliance and should not cannibalize other areas that will promulgate an effective overall compliance program.

# Reporting

Reporting within the compliance department holds a pivotal role in the overarching governance framework of an organization. Effective and detailed reporting not only ensures that compliance risks are communicated clearly across various levels of the organization but also provides a platform for compliance to demonstrate its intrinsic value. Far from being merely a cost center, a well-organized compliance report highlights the protective and enabling role that compliance plays, safeguarding the organization against regulatory pitfalls and enhancing business operations through risk management. This is essential in changing the perception of compliance from a "cost" to a strategic asset. The upcoming chapter will delve into basic strategies for reporting to senior management, boards, various committees, and other departments, emphasizing how tailored reporting can serve different organizational needs and decision-making processes.

The chapter will also explore the nuances of external reporting to regulators, auditors, and, where relevant, clients. External reporting requires not only accuracy but also adherence to specific regulatory standards and formats. This aspect of compliance reporting ensures that the organization maintains transparency with external stakeholders, meets regulatory demands, and builds trust by demonstrating accountability and diligence in its operations. Effective external reporting can mitigate risks of non-compliance penalties and foster stronger relationships with regulatory bodies. By outlining the procedures and best practices for external communication, the chapter aims to equip compliance professionals with the tools necessary to handle external pressures and requirements efficiently.

Lastly, the chapter will cover the integration of advanced data analytics and dashboard technologies in compliance reporting. Utilizing both quantitative and qualitative data, modern compliance departments can create dynamic, real-time dashboards that provide a clear view of the organization's compliance status at a glance. These tools not only streamline the process of monitoring compliance metrics but also enhance decision-making by providing comprehensive insights into trends, patterns, and potential areas of concern. This section will argue for the use of these technologies as a means to elevate the compliance function further, transforming raw data into strategic insights. By embracing these innovative reporting mechanisms, compliance professionals can better communicate the effectiveness of their programs both within the organization and to external stakeholders, thereby reinforcing the value of compliance in supporting and securing the organization's objectives.

## What to Report

Before we delve into the specifics of internal and external reporting, we should discuss what information should be reported. Using the Fundamentals of Compliance takes a lot of guesswork out of the equation as it provides a large amount of data to keep others informed of the compliance program.

Annual reporting on the compliance risk assessment and its outputs is crucial for maintaining a robust compliance framework within an organization. This report should particularly focus on areas where residual risks have intensified over time or where internal controls have shown repeated failures. Effective communication of these risks is essential; therefore, summarizing key risks in a concise manner, displaying them in graphical formats, and tracking trends over time can significantly enhance the comprehensiveness and clarity of the reports. For upper management and board members, it is advisable to emphasize the most critical risks or those with high residual risks. This level of prioritization helps senior leaders focus on the most significant threats to the organization, facilitating strategic decision-making and resource allocation.

Reporting should include updates on any changes in policies, which is essential for keeping the management looped into how regulatory updates are translating into operational adjustments. It is also important to detail the training conducted to ensure adherence to these new policies, providing management with insights into compliance levels and areas needing further attention. Additionally, when regulatory changes occur, the reports should discuss their impact on the organization, outline the adaptation process, and establish a clear timeline for the expected implementations. Identifying accountable owners for each change and assessing the impact magnitude are critical to ensure clear responsibility and expectation to management.

Furthermore, the organization's annual monitoring and testing plan should be reported annually, with the results reported quarterly. This keeps senior management regularly informed about the ongoing compliance activities and any issues that have been uncovered, ensuring there is continuous oversight and timely intervention. It is also important to include detailed data and analysis of the remediation efforts undertaken for issues identified in previous assessments.

Reporting on regulatory examinations is also crucial; such communications should detail the interactions with regulators, findings, and any required follow-up actions. This ensures that management is fully aware of the regulatory landscape and the organization's compliance status, which is vital for maintaining operational integrity and regulatory goodwill.

Here is a detailed list of items to consider reporting on:

• Risk Assessments

* Regulatory Change Management

* Policy changes and training on policies

* Monitoring and testing plan

* Results of monitoring and testing activities

* Tracking of remediation efforts

* Regulatory examinations

* Tracking of exam finding remediations

Of course, there may be other departmental aspects you may wish to include, for example, changes in headcount or current open requisitions. Meeting with senior management to see what information they may also find valuable is important as well. There may be aspects of regulation or compliance which they are focused on. If that is the case, you should make sure to communicate on those with some regularity.

## Internal Reporting

## Senior Management

Regular presentations of the compliance program to senior management, such as the CEO, General Counsel, or other top executives, are vital to ensuring that leadership is continually engaged with and informed about compliance activities and risks. Given the demanding schedules of these leaders, it is imperative to structure these presentations to convey essential information efficiently. Quarterly updates are recommended as they strike a balance between providing timely updates and allowing enough time for significant developments to occur that merit discussion.

When preparing these presentations, it is crucial to include executive summaries that distill the most critical risks or significant events from the period in question. These summaries should highlight key points and decisions needed, allowing senior management to quickly grasp the most pressing issues without needing to delve into granular details. The use of clear, concise language and bullet points can aid in emphasizing these critical risks and necessary actions.

Moreover, the reporting process should be interactive and adaptive. Compliance reports should evolve based on the feedback from previous presentations and changing organizational needs or external factors. Incorporating graphical information, such as charts, graphs, and heat maps, can greatly enhance the comprehensibility and impact of the data presented. Visual aids help in illustrating trends, comparisons, and progress in a way that is quickly understandable, facilitating informed decision-making. Remember, effective leaders make data-driven decisions, and they expect the compliance function to align with this approach by providing clear, actionable data. Thus, ensuring your reports are data-centric and visually engaging will help maintain the attention and support of busy executives, fostering a stronger compliance culture within the organization.

<u>Committees</u>

Compliance professionals often play crucial roles in various organizational committees, either as active members or as advisors. When involved in such capacities, it is essential that the compliance reports presented are meticulously tailored to align with the specific committee's purpose and charter. For instance, providing detailed information on privacy monitoring to an Investment Committee would not only be irrelevant but could also diminish the perceived value and credibility of the compliance function. Therefore,

<u>Interdepartmental Communication</u>

Sharing data and metrics from compliance reports with department heads and other key stakeholders is crucial for fostering a culture of transparency and collaboration within an organization. While these communications may be less formal than those prepared for the board or senior management, they are no less important. Regularly disseminating this information helps prevent departments from being unexpectedly labeled as high-risk and allows them to proactively address potential compliance issues. Such openness not only aids in early detection and mitigation of risks but also reinforces the role of the compliance function as a partner rather than a watchdog.

In the ongoing operations of a compliance program, which include conducting risk assessments, performing monitoring and testing, or facilitating examinations, maintaining constant contact with various departments is essential. This continuous engagement ensures that no piece of information comes as a surprise. Building trust across the organization is vital for compliance to be seen as a respected and integral part of the team. For instance, when developing a compliance dashboard, soliciting input from different departments can be highly beneficial. Asking for their preferences on what information they need and how they would like it presented not only tailors the dashboard to be more useful but also involves them actively in the compliance process.

However, it is important to recognize the sensitivity of some of the information handled by compliance. While fostering openness and sharing critical data, it is also necessary to ensure that any legally privileged or confidential information is carefully managed. This balance is key to maintaining legal compliance and protecting the organization's interests while still being as transparent as possible with internal stakeholders. Be clear about what information can be shared and what must remain confidential, and always be willing to explain the reasons for these distinctions. This approach not only respects legal boundaries but also enhances the credibility and reliability of the compliance function within the organization.

## External

## Regulators

Reporting information to regulators, whether mandated by law or as a proactive measure, requires meticulous attention to detail and a strategic approach to communication. In cases where regulatory reporting is compulsory, the data typically involves specifics about business activities or holdings that are critical to transparency and regulatory compliance. To ensure the integrity and accuracy of such data, organizations must implement well-defined procedures that include thorough quality assurance checks. These procedures are essential because inaccuracies in regulatory filings are often targeted by regulators as breaches of compliance, potentially leading to enforcement actions. Organizations must prioritize precision in their reporting processes to avoid these pitfalls, which can be costly and damaging to their reputation.

When it comes to reporting significant events or issues voluntarily to regulators, the approach must be even more considered and cautious. It is vital to meticulously scrutinize the language used in such communications to ensure it is fact-based and unambiguous. In instances where the content of the report could be particularly detrimental to the organization, it may be prudent to engage outside counsel. These legal experts can provide valuable guidance on how to frame the communication to mitigate potential negative repercussions while complying with regulatory requirements. This step is crucial because any negative report can prompt a regulator to initiate an examination or enforcement action, which can have significant implications for the organization.

In voluntary reporting scenarios, compliance plays a critical advisory role. It is important for compliance to be involved throughout the reporting process to ensure that all communications are accurate, complete, and appropriately vetted. Furthermore, before any significant communication is sent to a regulator, it should be discussed and agreed upon with all parties impacted by the potential fallout, including senior leadership. This "socialization" of the message ensures that everyone understands the potential consequences and is prepared for any regulatory response. By integrating compliance into these communications and decision-making processes, organizations can better manage their regulatory relationships and mitigate the risks associated with reporting.

Auditors

Reporting information to external auditors requires a high level of diligence, akin to the care taken when voluntarily reporting to regulators. The information shared must be characterized by its accuracy and completeness to avoid misrepresentations or omissions that could mislead auditors and regulators. This involves rigorous data verification and validation processes to ensure that all disclosed information is factual and comprehensive.

Timeliness is another crucial factor in reporting to external auditors. Reports should be submitted according to the agreed schedules, and any significant issues or findings should be communicated promptly. This not only facilitates a smooth audit process but also reflects the organization's commitment to transparency and compliance.

The context and explanation accompanying the data are equally important. Providing clear, concise background information helps auditors understand the framework within which the data was generated and its relevance to the audit. This should include an overview of the operational environment, any assumptions made during data compilation, and the methodologies used.

Before any information is disclosed to external auditors, it is essential to consult with the legal department. This precaution ensures that all communications are compliant with legal and regulatory requirements and that the organization's interests are safeguarded. Legal counsel can provide valuable insights into the implications of the data being reported and help craft the message in a legally sound manner. It is also advisable to engage with stakeholders impacted by the audit findings and senior management before and after reporting to auditors. This engagement ensures that all parties are aware of potential issues and the organization's response strategies, fostering a unified approach to addressing audit outcomes.

Maintaining a proactive relationship with external auditors is integral to effective corporate governance. This includes regular updates and sharing information similar to what is reported to regulators, thereby reinforcing the organization's commitment to transparency and accountability. Such proactive communications can build trust and facilitate a more collaborative and efficient audit process.

<u>Clients</u>

When compliance violations are discovered, the impact on clients can vary significantly, ranging from data breaches and privacy violations to over-billing or regulatory enforcement actions. Most jurisdictions mandate that affected clients must be informed about these incidents, which requires issuing formal notices. Although the task of preparing these notices often falls to departments like marketing, communications, or sales, it is crucial for the compliance team to be actively involved in crafting the content of these communications.

The role of compliance in this context is to ensure that the messaging is transparent and straightforward. In scenarios where other departments might be inclined to "spin" the message or minimize the perceived impact, compliance must advocate for a forthright approach. This involves clearly outlining the nature of the violation, the steps taken to address it, and any ongoing remediation efforts. Moreover, it is essential to discuss any potential remuneration that may be offered to affected clients to rectify the situation.

Providing direct contact within the organization is also beneficial. This contact should be someone who can address client concerns and provide further information if needed. Such a measure not only demonstrates the organization's commitment to resolving the issue but also builds trust with clients by showing that the organization is accessible and responsive.

The accuracy of these communications cannot be overstated, as they will be closely scrutinized by regulators. Any discrepancies or misleading information can lead to additional regulatory penalties and damage to the organization's reputation. Therefore, compliance must ensure that all client notifications are vetted for accuracy, completeness, and compliance with legal standards. This approach helps safeguard the organization against further legal complications and maintains its integrity in the eyes of clients and regulators alike.

## Creating and Building Dashboards for Reporting

The role of data within compliance departments has dramatically evolved with the advancement of technology. In earlier times, before the widespread adoption of digital tools, compliance officers often relied on manual methods to gather, tabulate, and analyze information. This process was not only time-consuming but also prone to human error, making it difficult to efficiently track and trend compliance-related data.

Today, the landscape has changed significantly with the availability of various technological tools that can automate and streamline these processes. Modern compliance departments can now utilize software to create dynamic and customizable dashboards. These dashboards serve as powerful tools, providing real-time data visualizations that help compliance professionals monitor, track, and analyze information more efficiently.

The adoption of such tools, like Microsoft Excel and Power BI, has been a game changer. Excel allows for versatile data manipulation and analysis with functions suited for detailed tracking and trending. Power BI, on the other hand, offers advanced data aggregation, visualization, and reporting features that can handle complex datasets and produce intuitive dashboards. These dashboards can be tailored to meet the specific needs of different stakeholders, making them extremely valuable for both internal and external reporting.

Compliance departments should actively seek to implement these dashboards as they not only enhance reporting capabilities but also play a crucial role in identifying potential areas of risk. By leveraging real-time data, compliance officers can quickly spot trends, outliers, and patterns that may indicate compliance issues or vulnerabilities within the organization.

Furthermore, these tools enable compliance professionals to provide timely and accurate data to various interested parties, including regulatory bodies, senior management, and other internal departments. This capability to swiftly report and share insights can significantly enhance an organization's ability to respond to compliance challenges and maintain regulatory compliance.

The integration of advanced data analytics tools into compliance strategies is essential for modern organizations. By adopting such technologies, compliance departments can enhance their operational efficiency, improve risk management, and strengthen their overall compliance posture.

Here's a list of essential data and metrics that compliance departments should consider monitoring regardless of industry:

1. Regulatory Compliance Rate: Measures the extent to which the organization complies with relevant laws and regulations. This can be broken down by department, region, or type of regulation and should originate from monitoring and testing findings or regulatory findings.

2. Audit Findings: Tracks the number and severity of deficiencies found during internal and external audits. This metric can help identify areas where internal control processes may need strengthening.

3. Compliance Training Completion: Percentage of employees who have completed mandatory compliance training. This ensures that staff is knowledgeable about compliance requirements and corporate policies.

4. Incident Reports: The number of compliance-related incidents reported, including breaches of conduct, ethical violations, and security lapses. Monitoring trends in this metric can help identify areas of risk.

5. Corrective Actions: Tracks the resolution of compliance issues, including the time taken to resolve such issues. This metric evaluates the efficiency and effectiveness of the response to compliance failures.

6. Risk Assessment Coverage: Percentage of business operations reviewed under the risk assessment program. This metric helps ensure that all potential risks are periodically reviewed and managed.

7. Employee Feedback: Data from surveys and feedback forms that gauge employee perceptions of the organization's ethical climate and adherence to compliance standards. This can provide insights into potential areas of non-compliance that might not be evident from other data sources.

8. Whistleblower Reports: Number of reports received from whistleblowers, which can serve as an early warning system for compliance issues.

9. Regulatory Fines and Penalties: Tracks the amount and frequency of fines and penalties levied against the organization for non-compliance. This can indicate the financial impact of compliance failures.

10. Third-Party Compliance: Assessment of compliance status of vendors, suppliers, and partners, especially important for industries with extensive outsourcing or supply chains.

11. Legal and Compliance Costs: Monitoring the costs associated with maintaining compliance, including legal fees, consulting fees, and costs of compliance-related modifications to business practices.

12. Compliance Policy Updates: Number and nature of updates made to compliance policies and procedures, reflecting the organization's responsiveness to changing regulatory environments.

These metrics should ideally be tracked using a compliance dashboard that allows for real-time monitoring and reporting. Tailoring these metrics to specific industry needs and regulatory requirements will enhance their relevance and utility in maintaining organizational compliance. As a compliance professional, you should try to get as much compliance data as possible. Think about all of the sources and seek to plug into them to extract information that can help you build a rigorous compliance program. This dashboard can act as a function of your compliance monitoring program and also help in developing reporting mechanisms.

# Advice

Now that we have covered the five Fundamentals of Compliance, lets discuss the final one, advice.  As we covered in the last chapter on Reporting, the information discussed or reported then flows back into the risk assessment to be used as data to determine the inherent rating and/or the control effectiveness.  Having knowledge of these events will help any compliance officer give good advice. In fact, knowing information from all of the Fundamentals is vital to providing good advice.

Let's discuss a hypothetical scenario: say you are sitting at your desk when the head of product innovation approaches you.  They want to discuss a new product offering that will be based on a current strategy but slightly changed to meet perceived market demand.  For this hypothetical, let's say you work at an asset manager.  The product manager wants to take a current existing strategy, long-term value investing (investing in stocks for the long term which have low price-to-book ratios), and add a layer of Environmental, Social, and Governance (ESG) to its strategy by excluding certain industries (e.g. weapons, mining, etc.).  As a compliance professional, you should be aware of the inherent risks associated with this type of product, including any regulatory priorities (for example, the SEC is currently focused on ESG in asset management).  You should also be aware of the policies and procedures surrounding portfolio management and the marketing of strategies.  Having a good understanding of what has, or will be, monitored/tested and what issues have been uncovered during past activities, including whether they have been remediated properly.  Additionally, it is important to know whether past regulatory examinations have resulted in findings and what information has been reported to management or other areas of the organization.  Drawing on this knowledge will allow you to provide sound advice to the product manager.  This advice would likely identify the priority of the SEC and discuss guidance on how the strategy should be marketed and what kind of records will need to be maintained in order to corroborate the ESG part of the strategy. Additionally, what kind of training may be needed to be implemented to assist in ensuring everyone who is part of the product launch is aware of the policies and procedures. Giving advice is a central function of compliance and is genuinely done on a daily basis.

Aside from drawing on the Fundamentals, it is recommended to give advice based on the following factors and this priority:

1) What does the policy state?

2) What does the rule require?

3) What are other market participants doing?

Answering these three questions will likely help you in providing sound advice. They may not always give an answer, say there is no policy, or the rule is silent on the type of activity you are being asked about? That is why it is important to network among your peers outside of your organization to be able to ask for advice.

What happens if you give bad advice? Or find out later that your previous position was wrong? This happens. You can never expect to be right all the time. I would also caution on avoiding "analysis paralysis" as some have coined. Overly researching an answer can lead to frustration from your counterparts seeking advice. If you happen to give bad advice the first thing you should do is own up to the mistake and contact the party immediately and let them know you made a mistake. This is difficult. No one wants to admit to making mistake, especially if your advice has already been acted on. However, trying to cover it up will only make matters worse. In a best-case scenario, you will be able to provide the correct advice. However, if that is not possible, tell the person(s) that you need more time, but be specific and try to act fast. Use the mistake as a learning experience, trying to pinpoint what may have caused the bad advice and work to avoid it in the future.

Networking within the compliance profession is a must. There are several associations and organizations in the marketplace to assist with that. For example, the Society or Corporate Compliance and Ethics (SCCE), the National Society of Compliance Professionals (NSCP), International Compliance Professionals Association (ICPA), International Association of Risk and Compliance Professionals (IARCP), and many others. If you are having difficulty finding an organization reach out to your industry peers on LinkedIn and ask to speak or meet if in the same area. This is not the time to be meek. There may come a time when you would want to discuss a situation or problem. Also, this is not a one-way street, offer to be a sounding board if the other person is seeking one. Networking has many professional benefits and expands your circle of knowledge. It is key to have these types of relationships in order to be successful in the profession.

Professional networking in the compliance profession offers several valuable benefits that can enhance both personal growth and professional opportunities. Here are some key advantages:

1. Knowledge Sharing and Learning: The field of compliance is continually evolving with new regulations, technologies, and best practices. Networking allows professionals to share knowledge and stay updated on these changes, providing opportunities for continuous learning and professional development.

2. Career Opportunities: Building a robust network can open doors to job opportunities that might not be advertised publicly. Many positions are filled through referrals and recommendations within professional networks. Being well-connected increases the likelihood of being considered for these roles.

3. Mentorship and Guidance: Networking can connect individuals with more experienced professionals who can offer mentorship and guidance. This can be particularly valuable in navigating the complexities and ethical dilemmas often encountered in compliance roles.

4. Enhanced Problem Solving: Compliance professionals often face unique challenges that require specialized solutions. Networking can provide access to a broader pool of resources and expertise, facilitating better problem-solving through collaborative approaches.

5. Professional Reputation: Active networking and participation in professional circles can help build and maintain a positive reputation within the industry. This is crucial in compliance, where trust and integrity are paramount.

6. Advocacy and Influence: Being connected with other professionals in the field can lead to opportunities to influence industry standards and regulatory practices. Networking can also provide a platform for advocacy on important issues within the profession.

7. Support and Resilience: A strong network can offer support during challenging times, such as navigating career transitions or dealing with complex compliance issues. This support can be instrumental in building resilience and maintaining motivation.

8. Access to Resources and Tools:*Networking can provide insights into effective tools, technologies, and strategies that other compliance professionals use, which can enhance the efficiency and effectiveness of one's own compliance practices.

Overall, networking in the compliance profession not only enhances personal and professional growth but also contributes to the effectiveness and integrity of the compliance function within organizations. I can't stress how important networking is as a compliance professional. It has assisted me on countless occasions and also provided me with some great friendships. Aside from networking it may also be of assistance to go to outside counsel or consultants.

<u>Asking for Help from Outside the Organization</u>

There are circumstances when the complexity or specificity of a regulatory issue goes beyond the internal capabilities of the compliance team. In such situations, turning to outside counsel or consultants becomes not only advantageous but necessary.

When to Seek Outside Counsel

1. Specialized Expertise: Regulatory landscapes can be highly specialized, such as those in finance, healthcare, or international trade. When facing niche issues that require deep domain knowledge, outside experts can provide the necessary insights and guidance that may not be available in-house.

2. Objective Assessment: External consultants can offer a fresh, unbiased perspective on compliance issues. This is particularly valuable in sensitive situations where internal politics or biases might influence the decision-making process.

3. Resource Constraints: During periods of high demand, such as a major compliance project or an unexpected regulatory inquiry, the internal team may lack sufficient resources to effectively handle the workload. Outside counsel can fill these gaps, ensuring that compliance efforts are sustained without compromising quality.

4. Legal Precedents and Updates: Compliance is a dynamic field with frequent updates to laws and regulations. External advisors stay abreast of these changes and can provide critical updates and training to ensure the organization remains compliant.

5. During Enforcement Actions: As discussed in the Chapter Issues and Examinations, outside counsel should always be sought for potential enforcement actions, given the procedural complexity.

Advocating for Outside Advice

Compliance professionals must be adept at advocating for the allocation of funds towards hiring outside counsel. Here's how they can effectively make their case:

1. Risk vs. Reward: Clearly articulate the potential risks of non-compliance versus the cost of hiring external advisors. Highlighting past instances where external advice has mitigated significant risks can be a persuasive argument.

2. Cost-Benefit Analysis: Provide a detailed cost-benefit analysis showing how external expertise could potentially save the company from expensive legal challenges, fines, or damaged reputations in the future.

3. Expert Testimonials and Case Studies: Presenting testimonials and case studies from other organizations that have successfully leveraged outside counsel can demonstrate the tangible benefits and practicality of such an approach.

4. Strategic Planning: Include the need for external consultants in the strategic planning phase of major projects or compliance calendar events. This proactive approach helps ensure that funds are allocated in the budget well in advance.

5. Compliance as an Investment: Frame compliance spending as an investment in the company's future, emphasizing how such investments protect and enhance the company's value and credibility.

Ultimately, the decision to seek outside counsel should be based on a strategic assessment of the organization's needs, potential risks, and the inherent capabilities of the in-house compliance team. By effectively advocating for the judicious use of external resources, compliance professionals can enhance their organization's ability to navigate complex regulatory environments safely and successfully.

Going to outside consultants can be an equally important strategy for compliance professionals seeking to enhance their organization's compliance framework. Outside consultants offer specialized services that can complement the work of an in-house compliance team in several critical ways.

Why Consider Outside Consultants

1. Technical Expertise: Outside consultants often bring specific technical expertise that may not exist within the organization. For instance, in areas like data protection, cybersecurity, and environmental compliance, the technical details can be intricate and constantly evolving. Consultants specializing in these fields can provide the necessary expertise to navigate these complexities.

2. Compliance Audits: External consultants can conduct thorough compliance audits to identify gaps in the organization's current compliance framework. Their independent status helps ensure that the audit results are unbiased, providing a clear picture of where improvements are needed. These mock audits can be very useful and should be a regular part of a good program.

3. Training and Development: Compliance is an area where continuous employee education and training are critical. Consultants can develop and deliver training programs tailored to the needs of the organization, ensuring that all employees are up-to-date with the latest regulatory requirements and best practices.

4. Crisis Management: In the event of a compliance breach or a regulatory investigation, outside consultants can provide the

necessary crisis management expertise. They help in managing the situation by advising on legal requirements, communicating with regulators, and implementing corrective measures to mitigate damage.

Advocating for Hiring Outside Consultants

When advocating for the engagement of outside consultants, compliance professionals should approach the decision-making process with clear strategies:

1. Demonstrate Specific Needs: Specify the particular areas where the consultants' expertise is needed. This could be for implementing new technology, addressing a gap in current expertise, or managing an upcoming regulatory change.

2. Highlight Flexibility and Cost Efficiency: Emphasize that consultants can be engaged on a project basis, which offers flexibility and can be more cost-effective compared to hiring full-time specialized staff.

3. Showcase Return on Investment (ROI): Prepare a detailed analysis showing how the consultants' interventions could lead to improvements in compliance processes, reductions in potential fines or legal costs, and enhanced operational efficiency.

4. Leverage Success Stories: Share examples from within or outside the industry where consultants have provided significant value in bolstering compliance programs. Real-world examples can help illustrate potential benefits and reassure stakeholders of the value brought by consultants.

5. Strategic Alignment: Align the need for consultants with the organization's strategic goals. Demonstrating how they help achieve broader business objectives can make a compelling case for their engagement.

By effectively utilizing outside consultants, compliance professionals can strengthen their organization's compliance efforts, ensuring not only adherence to regulations but also promoting a culture of integrity and ethical behavior across the organization.

In conclusion, Advice plays a major role in a compliance professionals day to day role. This chapter has emphasized the critical nature of leveraging information from risk assessments, policies and procedures, training programs, monitoring and testing mechanisms, issue remediation strategies, examinations, and reporting systems. Giving good advice helps build credibility and trust across the organization in the compliance program. Avoid becoming the department of "No." Work with your business partners to achieve their goals in a compliant manner. Usually, there is a way to achieve the objective while remaining compliant. Granted, it may require additional steps to be taken and controls put into place, but it is likely you can get to "Yes." There may be times when something is outright prohibited or against policy, and that is when a "No" is appropriate. But be mindful of these, as they should not represent a majority of your responses. Giving advice always leaves some room for error. If you happen to make a mistake, give yourself some grace; everyone has been there. Having an unrealistic expectation of being accurate one hundred percent of the time is simply not realistic nor human. Remember that there is a difference between knowledge and wisdom, so continually seek to learn and grow from advice given.

# Conclusion

Integrating the Fundamentals of Compliance for a Robust Compliance Program

As we reach the conclusion of "The Fundamentals of Compliance," it is essential to reflect on the interconnectedness of the core elements we have explored throughout this book. The chapters on "Risk Assessments," "Policies, Procedures, and Training," "Monitoring and Testing," "Issues and Examinations," "Reporting," and "Advice" each play a critical role in the tapestry of compliance. Together, they form a comprehensive framework that can be adapted to any industry across the globe, ensuring that organizations not only meet regulatory requirements but also uphold ethical standards and maintain public trust.

Risk Assessments: The cornerstone of any effective compliance program, risk assessments provide the insights needed to understand and mitigate potential threats. These assessments allow organizations to preemptively address areas of concern and tailor their compliance efforts to specific risks inherent in their operations. This is where all compliance programs should begin.

Policies, Procedures, and Training: Clearly articulated policies and procedures establish the framework for compliant behavior within an organization. Coupled with robust training programs, ensure that every member of the organization understands their compliance obligations and how to fulfill them, thus embedding compliance into the corporate culture.

Monitoring and Testing: To verify that policies and procedures are not only understood but also effectively implemented, ongoing monitoring and testing are imperative. These activities help identify compliance gaps and inefficiencies in real-time, allowing for corrective action to be taken.

Issues and Examinations: Recognizing and resolving compliance issues promptly is crucial to maintaining the integrity of an organization's compliance program. Regular internal and external examinations provide an additional layer of oversight, ensuring that compliance practices not only meet current standards but are also continuously improved upon.

Reporting: Transparent reporting mechanisms are essential for communicating the status and effectiveness of the compliance program to internal and external stakeholders. Effective reporting supports organizational accountability and provides a documented trail of efforts to comply with applicable laws and regulations.

Advice: Compliance is a dynamic field influenced by changes in laws, technology, and market conditions. Continuous professional advice and guidance are necessary to navigate these complexities, ensuring that the compliance program remains relevant and effective. Drawing on the information and outputs from the above Fundamentals, arm a compliance professional with the right knowledge to give sound advice.

In crafting an effective compliance program, it is important to recognize that these elements are not isolated silos but are deeply interdependent. The strength of a compliance program lies in its ability to integrate these components seamlessly, creating a resilient structure that adapts to evolving regulatory landscapes and industry practices. These practices should be continually enhanced as they feed into one another.

As the global business environment continues to evolve, so too must our approaches to compliance. The fundamentals outlined in this book provide a blueprint for building and maintaining a compliance program that not only prevents misconduct and ensures legal adherence but also fosters a culture of ethical integrity. This is not merely a regulatory requirement but a strategic advantage that can distinguish a company in its field, enhance its reputation, and secure its long-term success. If you are starting from a blank page, allow yourself some time to build out these practices, being keenly aware that enhancements should continuously be made. No program is perfect.

In conclusion, the principles detailed in "The Fundamentals of Compliance" are applicable across any industry worldwide. They are designed to provide organizations with the knowledge and tools needed to establish a robust compliance framework, one that not only withstands scrutiny but also supports sustainable, ethical business practices. As such, every stakeholder engaged in the creation, implementation, and oversight of compliance activities is empowered to contribute to a culture of compliance that is both effective and enduring.

Thank you for taking the time to read this. I welcome your feedback and discussion on the Fundamentals of Compliance. You can connect with me on LinkedIn at

www.linkedin.com/in/jamesrdowning/. I am always open to discussing where you might disagree or whether you have different ideas! Compliance is a passion of mine and I always welcome a conversation.

# James Downing Bio:

James Downing has 20+ years of experience in Compliance in the broker dealer, investment advisory and investment company industries. James has held several senior leadership roles as Chief Compliance Officer in various organizations in the financial services industry. Prior to working in the public sector James was a FINRA examiner from the Chicago District Office for 5 years. James has his Juris Doctorate with honors from Taft Law School and a Master of Accounting with honors from Roosevelt University. James has his series 7, 24, 27, 53, and 66 from FINRA. Jim actively participates on several NSCP committees and was formerly the Chair of the Board.